TRUMPETS
AND ROARS

TRUMPETS AND ROARS

SAROJ K. PATNAIK

PARTRIDGE

To order additional copies of this book, contact
Partridge India
000 800 10062 62
orders.india@partridgepublishing.com

www.partridgepublishing.com/india

CONTENTS

NATIONAL TIGER CONSERVATION AUTHORITY

(Statutory Body under Ministry of Environment, Forest and Climate Change, Govt. of India)

BISAN SINGH BONAL
Addl. DGF (Project Tiger) &
Member Secretary (NTCA)

FOREWORD

I am happy to know that Shri Saroj K. Patnaik has written a book titled "Trumpets and Roars" based on his long experience in working for wildlife conservation and management of the country as head of wildlife wing of a state. He has long standing experience of working in wildlife management in different capacities during his service and after his retirement as well, spanning over more than half a century.

I have gone through few articles of the book which I find often thrilling and absorbing while conveying simple conservation messages to the readers. Many articles deal with conservation of tropical forests and are quite inspiring. As there are very few popular books written in lucid and reader friendly style on this subject, I hope that this will be well received by all readers in India and abroad.

(B.S. Bonal)

Addl. Director General (Wildlife/Project Tiger) &
Member Secretary,
National Tiger Conservation Authority, India
23.01.2017

ACKNOWLEDGEMENT

While writing this book "Trumpets and Roars", the first people who come to my mind are the field forest staff of my state and those of the entire country, who work tirelessly often in very difficult conditions. I shall be failing in my duties if I do not acknowledge the guidance and encouragement I received from Late Padmashree Saroj Raj Choudhury during my brief interaction with him, which gave me strength to peruse wildlife management as a passion in the later part of my service career and thereafter. I gratefully acknowledge the contribution those about whom I have mentioned in the book and some I have not been able to. Sri K.L. Purohit has painstakingly retrieved some old photographs used in the book and allowed me to print them. Sri Rajkumar Behera has voluntarily taken pains to draw some sketches for the book. I sincerely acknowledge his contribution. I also acknowledge contribution of Sri Rajesh Kumar Mohapatra for his help in editing the proof.

I owe my gratitude to my wife Manju, who inspired me to write the book.

Saroj K. Patnaik

TUSKER OF TARINIBILA

It was a January afternoon deep inside Similipal National Park of Odisha state in eastern part of India, I was on a routine tour to this beautiful Tiger Reserve. This Tiger Reserve had been established 15 years back in 1973 as a part of a very ambitious programme to improve the status of tiger, which had fallen to a low of less than 1800 all over India. Similipal had only 17 of them. Selected as one of 9 reserves of the country to be given this status, this was headed by Sri Saroj Raj Choudhury as its first Field Director, after his teaching assignment in Dehradun, where he was responsible to lay the foundation of training on scientific wildlife management in the country, when he organized 6-month certificate course in Wildlife Management. Later on Sri Choudhury reared a tigress Khairi and has given deep insight to tiger behavior in his book 'Khairi the Beloved Tigress', which was hitherto unknown to science. He was awarded the prestigious award of *'Padmashree'* by the government of India after his death.

I was traveling in soft topped petrol driven green 'Gypsy', jeep with very low engine noise, which I was driving. My family consisting of my wife, two daughters and a son, driver, a Forester and a Forest Guard of the Tiger Project accompanied me. Similipal was getting chilly, as evening was fast approaching and shadows of the trees lengthening against the setting sun. Every one was savoring the sylvan beauty of the area. The call of the peafowl and a distant sambar stag and crocking of the red jungle fowl reverberated in the valley and was giving an impression of large number of animals giving alarm call simultaneously. As our vehicle's wheels crushed lemon grass tufts with luxuriant tillers growing between the wheel tracks of the forest road, it was emitting a sweet aroma of citrus. We were traveling in the 'core area' of the tiger reserve from Jenabill to go to Barakamuda through Tarinibila. Core area is designated to keep it free from the undue human interference in order to provide adequate privacy to the wild animals for feeding, socialising, mating and breeding. Even the tourists are not allowed to enter this area and movement of 'tiger project' staff was very limited. Though 4 small villages still existed there, it was the endeavor of the Govt. to relocate them out side the reserve to eliminate the biotic interference from the people living there and their cattle. The unpaved forest road with brownish soil on which we were traveling was following a hill stream on its left. On the right was a hillock, which had been cut to make the road through which my jeep was traveling at a fairly good speed, as the road surface was quite smooth, though it was narrow, intermittently stopping to ask the forest staff about animal signs, plants and distance to our destination. The dry leaves lying on the forest road presented a look of a multi colored carpet of yellow, deep red and rusty brown. They were making rustling sound when the wheels of the gypsy were crushing them as they passed over them. The portion between the two wheel tracks had knee-high lemon grass patches, making it almost impossible to see the road surface. The children were also very curious and were asking several questions regarding wild flowers, visibility of animals, about the life of the staff that quite often stay in this forest alone and endure a very harsh life. They wanted to know how they get their food stuff, how do they move in the forest alone, where there are lot of ferocious wild animals, what do they eat, how do they get treated when they go down with malaria and so on.

I was very alert, as this was the usual time for the animals, to move for foraging and going to the water holes. Of course, Similipal has large number of perennial streams, whose crystal clear water, thanks to its excellent vegetation cover, still more or less intact. This water is taken by wild animals, without depending on small water holes unlike in case of other drier areas of the country. This perhaps explains the cause of poor sighting of herbivores near water holes in Similipal Tiger Reserve as they are dispersed all along the streams without congregating around small pools. The high density of trees and dense under growth, caused due to high rainfall is other reason for sparse visibility of animals in this park. Meadows or openings are few except around the village areas, cultivated fields and few frost affected patches. The winter frost in some valleys kills all saplings leaving only few grass species which can stand this, thus creating vast meadows frequented by herbivores.

Tall and majestic Sal trees were casting their long shadows on the road. Orchids were hanging from many tree branches but were yet to bloom. The tree branches turn in to bouquets of colorful flowers in May when almost all species of orchids bloom. There are more than 100 varieties recorded from this reserve.

Number of single red jungle fowls crossed our road or took to flight after a short run with their ka-ka-k-k sound after being alarmed by the movement of our vehicle, pea fowls made deep throated alarm calls from tree tops hearing the sound of our vehicle, which echoed from all the other hillocks. Groups of Malabar giant squirrels, an arboreal animal jumped from one tree branch to the other, displaying their beautiful brown and black coat with yellowish white underbelly. This animal, being arboreal inhabits dense forests with close tree canopy to facilitate movement on branches with very occasional descent to the forest floor. My jeep negotiated several bends and crossed a small ridge to go to an arch shaped stretch of the road, when all of us spotted a huge young tusker speeding straight at us from the opposite direction. I applied sudden brake and the gypsy grinded to a halt but kept the ignition switch on, not to unduly alarm him. He also came to an abrupt halt. I didn't know if he could hear the sound of the jeep, saw it or smelt it. Elephant's sense of small is very strong, through vision and hearing are moderate. He gets the smell from long distance if the wind is blowing towards him.

I asked all the occupants of the vehicle to keep quiet and concentrate on the activity of the pachyderm. Children with their eyes wide open kept their attention glued to the tusker and breathed heavily. He was a majestic animal, about 2.7 meters tall, heavily built, with two equal and pointed tusks about half meter long with large ears. He was perhaps less than 30 years old, rather a young animal. Wild elephants' life span varies between 60 to70 years. While his head was darkish, the body looked dusty brown due to dust bath with brownish earth. Elephants quite often take dust bath with their trunk to keep away insects that torment them and also to cool themselves in hot months.

We (tusker and me) kept looking at each other. Though it was difficult for me to reverse, it was not impossible. But I decided not to reverse, as that could have encouraged him to give a chase, as he might think that I have retracted seeing him in front due to fear for him.

He also must have thought the same, as almost all animals are scared of man. Even tigers do not attack people for shake of attacking. They only attack as a measure of self-defense, when they feel that the enemy is about to attack and has crossed the critical distance. Only man-eaters do attack people unprovoked for flesh. They turn man-eaters when they cannot stalk a fast prey due to injury, old age or debility. In such situation livestock, humans or village dogs became easy targets for them due to their slow unsuspecting movement. Some times they learn killing of human beings and cattle from their parents.

I did not know what to do. Minutes passed by ... ten - fifteen – twenty-twenty five…….. As the slope of the hillock to his left was rather too steep and on his right was a deep precipitous depression leading to the stream, it was not easy for him to go to any side. Turning back would make him vulnerable to possible attack from my team, as would have been thought by him. He stood still; intermittently raising lower part of his trunk pointed at us, perhaps to get our smell and fanning his large ears.

I looked at him more closely particularly for the sign of *'musth'* fluid, which flows from either side of a tusker's temple when a 'tusker' or *'makhna'* (*'makhna'* is a male elephant without tusks) comes to *musth*. That is the time when the animal is sexually exited and remains so for about 2 to 3 weeks. At this time he looses mental balance. It occurs mostly in winter months among adult elephants. During this period the *mahauts* (keeper) of captive tuskers are most vulnerable to attack and many of them have been killed. I found that there was no secretion.

I inched forward towards him switching on to first gear, perhaps crossing 10 out of 40 meter distance between us in about 5 minutes. He concentrated hard on my approach without any movement and perhaps felt that I am determined to move on the road, but not dangerous as far as his safety is concerned. This of course, he might have already learnt by seeing several forest staff and vehicles on his usual rounds, which had never harmed him or his herds.

I further moved. He reversed by few steps still keeping his eyes glued on my jeep and gave out a short grunt and very cautiously climbed about 10 steps to his left on to the hill with difficulty and stood still with face turned to right towards the jeep. I could only see his body through the undergrowth of grasses and *Indigofera* (Giliri) bushes. An elephant can remain completely motionless and camouflage well when he needs to do so.

The tusker giving us a passage.

I realized that he had deliberately allowed us a safe passage. I thought I should not waste time any further. I pressed the accelerator hard and sped along the road. Occupants of the vehicle looked back and saw him slowly descending down to the road. Once back on the road, he followed us for about hundred meters perhaps to ensure that we are no longer a risk to his safety and then turned and sped to follow his route. The forest reverberated with cries of several peafowls, which were watching the pachyderm from their perches on the treetops.

Had he wanted to attack, we were very easy targets to be crushed. But the death of humans due to elephant attacks is quite common in all degraded elephant habitats including those in parts of Orissa, which has about 2000 elephants out of 25,000 – 30,000 elephants living in the wild in the country. Nearly 500 elephants live the Similipal and its adjoining areas of Kudiha of Baleswar district and Hadgarh of Keonjhar district, making it the largest elephant habitat of the State. But the human kill and depredation there is the least, because of the large forested tract over which the herds have freedom to move and feed. Elsewhere man has depleted the forests, cultivated crops along the routes called 'elephant corridors' followed by elephants in search of food, water and cover for generations. Townships, industries, mines and other projects have sprung up where the pachyderms were freely and fearlessly moving in the recent past. Thus these foraging and long ranging animals came to conflict with people, while they keep on moving long distances, without food and harassed by people. When they strike back, it is often fatal.

Hence, it is essential that we keep this gentle but powerful animal's habitat intact so that they continue to live in harmony with nature. In the process we protect our rich biodiversity, while enrich our much-needed ground water and provide vast carbon sinks to gobble up the pollutants generated by burning of fossil fuels. They are not only part of our heritage; they do help our environment through seed dispersal of different forest species. While in captivity, they are put to number of uses like logging, tourism, carrying men and goods through difficult terrain and so on. They are a part of our culture, mythology and history.

Can we not give this gentle animal a helping hand by leaving their habitat intact????

2

FOUR TOES AND A PAD

The dry leaves on the boulder strewn along the dry nala were being crushed under my hunter shoes and were producing a rustling sound much to our annoyance, as I was leading a team of forest field staff of Baliguda Forest Division of Odisha state through the deep forests of Eastern Ghats and a lone dove was letting out a monotonous call. The langurs on treetops were calling "Hoon-hoon-hoon" and "khe-khe-khe" perhaps sensing danger on that hot afternoon in May 1972. Such behaviour could have been triggered due to presence of my team deep inside this tropical deciduous forest, normally not frequented by people in this number in hot summer months or due to some predator which we could not see.

This visit was part of the first tiger census operation in India. Sri Saroj Raj Choudhury a forester from Orissa had just evolved tiger census techniques for the entire country. He was many years later honoured with Padmasri award posthumously for his contribution to the cause of wildlife conservation. Every tiger state of the country had been divided into several census units and training had been organized for all the field forest staff to take up the census work to know exact status of tiger for working out a conservation strategy for this majestic predator. Indirect evidences and information gathered from foresters in the country indicated that Indian tiger, also popularly known as Royal Bengal Tiger was very badly threatened in the country with an estimated number of less than 1800 animals left in the wild against an estimate of 40,000 in the beginning of the century and needed stringent protection measures urgently.

The technique assumed few facts. One of them is that a tiger must approach a water hole at least once in 24 hours to quench its thirst. The second being, like human finger prints the tiger's hind foot prints called 'pug marks' of each tiger differs from the other. The seven-day census operation involved collection of local information about tiger and leopard movements, locating all the water holes, which are very few in number in May, the driest month in Indian tropical forests. This was followed by erasing of all old marks around the water holes and then tracing out the outlines of the hind-right pugmark in a sheet of glass called 'tiger tracer' or pouring of 'Plaster of Paris' paste on a pugmark and allowing it to dry and then take this impression called 'plaster cast' for comparison with others from neighboring habitats to ascertain if the same animal has visited more than one waterhole during the day.

After training organized in all divisions for the staff, the forest field staff was quite keen to locate tigers in their respective territory. My area of operation was Balliguda Forest Division in Phulbani district of Orissa, earlier an agency area of Madras Presidency. It was a plateau with a mean elevation of at least 600 meters. I was nominated as Divisional Coordinator for the census operation.

Sri Hooda, the other Assistant Conservator of Forests of the Division sent massage to me that tiger pugmarks have been located by a tribal group who had been to the forest of Dharampur Reserved Forest for collecting fuel wood and the Forest Guard has visited the site near the waterhole and preserved the pugmarks with earthen pots and bamboo baskets. Mr. Hooda wanted me to go there immediately.

I never wanted to loose any time, as this was a very rare opportunity to locate the tiger pugmark. We were quite exited at the prospect. The jeep could hardly go for hundred meters from the main road and thereafter there was no road. We abandoned the jeep and started walking through the tropical deciduous forest of Sal, Bija, Asan, Kusum, Dhaura, Salai, Arjun, Sidha and Karada etc. It was about 11.00 a.m. and heat was intense, despite the altitude. The shades of few semi-evergreen trees like Jamun were quite soothing. Our team consisted of about 10 persons including forest staff and a few local tribals.

The team made quite speedy progress, through the forest crossing valleys, ridges, boulders and dry streams. All were quite tense and quiet as it was tiger country. Then we descended to a large dry stream full of rounded pebbles and larger boulders interspersed with big rocks, massive roots of Arjun trees. Sal, Asan, Dhaura, Kendu and Kusum trees lent different colours to the forest. While Kusum trees were draped with red to greenish red foliage, young sal leaves were shining green with white flowers. Fissured dark bark of Assam and Kendu contrasted with the light coloured bark of Arjun, Dhaura, Moi and Genduli. Sun light filtering through the closed canopy openings created bright spots on the ground mostly covered with shadows.

But our team concentrated on finding the pugmarks. Hours passed by. We paused for taking water from our water bottles and then proceeded. It was my first opportunity for a serious wildlife work after 7 years in state forest service, after graduating from the prestigious Indian Forest College, Dehradun. It was hard walking. Finally we came to a bowl shaped depression on the dry stream. It was a little pool 5 meters in length 3 meters wide, with about 0.5 m deep clear water in the middle of the depression. The Forester, Forest Guards and two tribal men rushed to see if the pots and baskets put on the pugmarks were all intact.

But to their dismay, the pots were all broken and baskets displaced. Who has done this? This was question in every ones mind. Has any one visited the spot and deliberately destroyed the evidence? We went closer. To our surprise animal footprints were everywhere. They were of tiger, cheetals, sambars, wildboars and birds. All animals frequent this pool of water being the only waterhole in kilometers. There were number of fresh pugmarks.

We looked all around the depression surrounded by big boulders and suddenly on the western side we saw streaks of fresh dried blood flowing down the rock face. Brown hair struck to the boulder surface and the coarse sand below was trampled as if a wrestling match had just taken place. I climbed to the top of the boulder, for getting a better view of all the boulders. To my surprise there were blood marks on many boulders and on one where there was a depression, there was little yellow fluid with white dried foam.

It did not take long for me to reconstruct the story. A drama must have been enacted here. As usual the herbivores must have come to the waterhole for taking water, when the royal cat would be lurking around. When he attacked the sambar, the animal, the largest of Indian deers has put up a lot of resistance, when all others have fled the site in panic. The tiger has dragged the big animal to take the body to the high ground to avoid slush and wet ground. It was perhaps too heavy. Finally he could lift the carcass to the top of the boulder. He had urinated nearby leaving its tell-a-tale mark of white incrustation around the yellow fluid. This has perhaps taken place in the early morning hours.

The blood mark led us to a cave like tunnel formation between two boulders, looking dark. It smelled of tiger all around. The Forester had a 5-cell torch, which he was about to focus into the cave. I stopped him, as this could be dangerous.

The Forester trying to see the cave.

My team was scared as the smell and signs of tiger were everywhere. I asked them to stay together and look for the best available pugmark on a drier ground on that fine sand. Finally few good impressions with four toes and pad was located. In case of tiger only four out of its five toes get impressed on the ground. A leopard pugmark is identical in shape to that of a tiger, though relatively much smaller. Unlike these cats, the pugmark impressions of hyena, wolf, jackal, fox and wild dogs have their nail mark impression at the tip of each toe as they cannot retract them. Once located, a tracing was made on the tiger tracer and 'Plaster of Paris' was made to slurry and poured on two pugmarks. They solidified in about fifteen minutes. We lifted them, wrote the date and place on the upper face and slowly traced our way back through the dry stream while keeping on looking back towards the entrance of the cave.

About 1 km. from there, a lone barking deer (Muntjack) barked looking at our team reassuring that we are no more close to the tiger.

A full-grown tiger takes about 80 cheetals or equal volume of other herbivore meat per year, that is about 1 cheetal or its equivalent in every 4- 5 days. After killing he sucks blood and then drags the animal to a safe place, where he keeps the carcass covered with soil, grasses and vegetation to keep it safe from scavenging animals like, hyena, jackal or vultures. He does not kill till he does not feel the need for killing due to hunger. Man or cattle perhaps fall at the end his order of preferences, as tiger is a sporting animal, which loves to stalk his prey, overpowers and kills it.

He takes to killing and eating slow moving animals like men and cattle, when either he is too old for hunting or has been injured due to any reason like snaring or trapping, shooting by arrows or percupine quills etc. Of course, once he starts killing human beings he continues to be a man-eater, transmitting also the same trait to her offsprings, if it is a female. Thus in order to save this species, saving its habitat and the pray population is important. Tiger is considered to be at the apex of the 'biological pyramid' of tropical Indian forest. If a pair of tiger is to thrive, they need at least 160-cheetal equivalent of prey population to be produced every year so that the base number, which is the capital remains intact. Of course much larger prey base is needed to support a breeding pair with its cubs. These herbivores also need enough vegetative edible biomass to support this population.

That census operation in 1972 arrived at a figure of about1800 tigers in the entire country and was the precursor to the launching of the 'Project Tiger' one of the most ambitious and successful conservation projects in the world. From 9 in 1973 the number of 'Tiger Reserves' in India has reached around 50 today. Though the population had shown a rising trend the number has shown drastic fall in the last decade or so. Fortunately in some reserves the situation is very encouraging in recent years. These projects are not only aimed at protecting the tigers, but also shall play a very important role in preserving the entire ecosystems, the prey population, other fauna and flora there. They shall also save the rich biodiversity in the protected areas from extinction and help recharge ground water while neutralizing air pollution, increasing every day due to burning of fossil fuel.

This majestic large cat needs your helping hand to survive, as other populations of tigers in other Asian countries are facing much more serious threat to their long term survival.

———————— ✦✦✦✦✦ ————————

3

EIGHT LEGS AND A TIGER

Our elephant carrying me and three other officers in a training programme with the 'Mahaut' was pushing though a dry river in a Central Indian Forest. Sunrise was still more than an hour away. Gradually as the sun was brightening the tree forms, banks of the dry river, the meadows flanking the river were becoming clearer. The *Cheetals* (spotted deer) those had taken rest in the meadows for the night to escape the attack from the predators like tigers and leopards lurking in the forest fringe were slowly rising to their feet. They had perhaps observed two elephants carrying us and the stag's eyes were glued to our group. He had raised his trail and was intermittently stamping his right fore leg and giving out an alarm call, to warn his herd of danger. A small herd of *barasinga* (hard footed swamp deer), an endangered species, had already started grazing. A herd of wild boars with their heads down hurried in front of our elephant to go back to their own shelter after the night round in search of food of roots and suckers.

It was a scene in the Kanha Tiger Reserve in Mandla district of Madhya Pradesh in early eighties when I was there with 15 other officers of the country for a training programme organized by the Wildlife Institute of India. By then Kanha National Park had already become an excellent protected area of the country. Given protection as a Vice royal Shooting Block under the British from 1926, this patch of forest had graduated in to a National Park. This was one of first lot of 9 Tiger Reserves of the country, which were established for giving special protection to tiger in 1973 as the global tiger population had fallen drastically. India's tiger population, though highest among all other range countries had plummeted to an estimated low of less than 1800.

As the pachyderms proceeded with their human cargo, mist of dawn started lifting as the skyline started becoming clearer. The birds on their perches on the tree branches, bushes and ground started their activity and the entire forest sprang to life with call of peafowl, jungle fowl, partridges, doves and flying parakeets in formations.

Breaking this cacophony came a distant piercing growl heavy and muffled. My ears registered this sound appearing to be coming almost from a direction between the front and right hand corner. It was unmistakably the roar of a tiger. None others including the *mahaut* could hear the roar, as they were busy chatting and perhaps very much absorbed in watching the transformation of the immediate surrounding from a sleepy forest expanse draped in the large white sheet of mist to one springing back to life with hectic activity, unfolding all its colours after being exposed to early morning sunlight. Some clicked their cameras.

I motioned to all our friends to maintain silence and told Ramdhin, the Mahaunt that I have clearly heard a tiger from the right hand direction. He did not believe and dismissed my version saying "Sir, it may be some other sound. I have not heard anything". But Randhin, based on his long experience of working here did keep quiet and waited for the next growl to confirm if at all I heard it correctly. I was very sure and communicated through sign language only, as I did not want any further distraction, as we may miss the next roar, if we do not concentrate.

There it was! A roar, loud and clear. It came from almost right hand side 15 minutes after the first. Ramdhin speeded up the elephant with the sign though his legs. Three tons of power broke in to gallop (or fast walk) and lumbered along and in no time climbed the steep bank of the rivulet and crossed a patch of tall grasses and a narrow meadow to a thicket of bamboos. The other elephant carrying other officers was left far behind.

As we got in to the bamboo forest, Ramdhin was cautious. With long experience of working in a prestigious park like Kanha, he knew that this is the area where the tiger might have made a kill and lurking somewhere, deftly camouflaging his tawny coat. Though he has never been trained in 'Wildlife Management', he knew pretty well that the transition zone between the opening or meadow and the thicker forest known as 'edge' is the zone where maximum wildlife activity takes place. This is because; the herbivores come to the open at night to be able to get protection from the predators, as they can see an attacking predator from a long distance. It is just in the fringe where the predators operate to get the advantage of cover. From there they take a leap on the unsuspecting stag and drag him to the cover, where they can keep the carcass beautifully concealed under vegetation and soil to protect it from the scavengers like hyena, jackals and vultures and eat for several days depending on the size of the animal hunted.

Our elephant was making her way through the bamboo clumps pushing the bamboos to either side with her strong trunk. She was taking cautious steps and stopping and raising her trunk to get the smell of the tiger, as perhaps she was getting the tiger smell much better due to the elephant's strong sense of smell. Despite their size and strength elephants do not take the tigers for granted as when encountered they give tough fight resulting in injury or sometimes death to one of them. Baby elephants are quite favorite prey of tigers.

Oh there he was, with a piercing look from under a bush, where he lied completely motionless. The body of the large cheetal stag with blood oozing from the neck was lying in a pool of blood about 3m away from the tiger. The kill was fresh, perhaps killed in the dawn just before we heard the growl.

Ramdhin was impatient. Perhaps he was keen to call his colleague 'Chander' on the other elephant. He blew his thunder whistle piercing though the bamboo thicket 3 times. Then came the reply from Chander from about 100 meters away. This indicated that he knew the position and is coming in that direction. This is a usual mode of short distance communication in the forest, when radio communication through very high frequency (VHF) walkie-talkie is not available.

This whistle perhaps disturbed the tiger, which got up and headed north majestically, while looking back at his kill and us. He moved about 30 meters to shade of a banyan tree and lied down there under its shade. We could barely see him through the sparse bamboo growth. While perhaps he wanted to maintain a safe distance from the elephants and us, he also was in no mood to abandon the kill, for which lot of efforts might have gone in to the entire operation. All chases after the prey are not usually successful. Though a tiger picks up very high speed while chasing a fast prey, he can maintain this for a very short distance, after which he slows down. Hence quite often the prey escapes.

Chander arrived with his elephant 'Sahjadi' followed by another elephant with Mr. Pantane the Deputy Director of the Park. All of us moved to an open ground close to the banyan tree, under which the tiger was resting. We were quite exited as very few of us had ever seen such a huge cat so close and for so long. He was lying down with his eyes partially open, placing his enormous head on his right forearm and giving a look of enjoying a slumber, oblivious of our presence. Sunlight filtered though the vegetation. We started taking photographs of the tiger. Perhaps we stayed there for more than an hour. The Central Indian summer sun became very bright and hot. We, who had left the camp at 4.00 am without bath, with only a cup of tea, were quite hungry and thirsty. We thought we should go back to the camp, as our return journey would take more than an hour. Our elephant was carrying Sri N.C. Patnaik,

Sri C. G. Mishra and in P.K. Mishra besides me, all senior forest officers. When we were about to leave, Mr. Pantane, told us to change the elephant, as he wanted to stay on at the site and our elephant "Basanti' was the most reliable among the lot for tracking the tigers.

We agreed. As the other elephant came parallel to Basanti I was first to go to the other elephant. I opened the iron rod, which was in our front and stood on the foot board and slowly put my feet on the foot board of the other 'hawda' of Shahjadi. To my surprise the foot board gave way and I came down to the ground. With a muffled thud my 70 kilogram body falls on the hard ground, between two elephants, with eight legs surrounding me. There was commotion, as all of them sitting on elephants became worried as to how to rescue me saying,' sher hai-sher hai'.

My first concern was my waist, which I felt that, might have been fractured from the two meters of sudden fall. I tried to lift myself from the ground and was relieved to find that there was no pain in any part of my body. I can get up without any support.

Commotion further mounted to express concern about my precarious position. I gestured them to maintain silence, as I knew that any uncalled for alarm, may provoke the tiger as well the 2 elephants. Either, the movement of any of eight massive legs may hurt me or the tiger could charge. I looked around to find an opening wide enough to escape from the confines of two elephants and their eight legs. My only route out appeared to be towards the hind side of both the pachyderms. But, while going out through this hind opening, I was going closer to the tiger. But there was no alternative. As I started doing that, there was again cry from my friends, 'Sher hai', meaning 'there is tiger'. I again prayed them for maintaining silence, while glancing at the tiger, which did not care even to look up. I took a small round to go to the front of Sahjadi, who slightly angled her foreleg and curved her trunk upward to facilitate my mounting onto the *howda* obeying instructions of Chander. I put my hunter shoes clad right foot firmly on the leg of the elephant holding her ear and put the other foot on her curved trunk, while Chander extended his hand to support me to mount the '*howda*'. I looked back at the tiger. He was still lying still, with occasional opening of his eye like a slit and slight movement of his ears. Two elephants still continued to stand there.

Being rescued.

My senior colleagues Mr. Patnaik and Mr. Mishra together spoke, 'Thank God, we all are again together'. As Shehjadi was walking carrying us back, I tried to feel if there was injury of any kind on my body, which I could not have noticed as everything went on too fast and then the immediate concern was safety than any other thing. There was none.

Everybody wandered as to why there was no reaction of this majestic large cat, when he found a very delicious pray just about 20 meters from him. Several reasons could be attributed to this. Tigers never hunt unless they are hungry or there is a need for hunting. All tigers are not man-eaters. They only take to human kills, when they are sick or injured, not to be able to stalk a fast prey or they inherit the trait from their mother or siblings. This tiger had just made a kill and the meal was still waiting for him. Besides, the presence of three elephants kept the cat glued to the place where he was lying. Though the elephant calves are a delicacy for tigers, they very rarely embark on such miss-adventure of attacking a sub adult or full grown elephant. In the wild it is often seen that the tigers follow the elephant herds having calves and keep waiting for the opportunity when the calves wonder away from the herd or stay behind, failing to keep pace with the rest of the herd. It strikes only then.

Another aspect that a field forester should always remember is that one should never panic. If you panic you have lost half the battle before the fight. While in panic, one cannot take a decision correctly. Everything shall then go wrong to your disadvantage. It is possible to overcome many odds if you stay calm and take decisions. All wild animal attacks are just not for killing. Quite often the attacks are in self-defense.

Most animals are scared of man. Hence one should not make any sudden movements or go too close to make him/her feel that he/she is threatened.

Because of fragmentation of tiger habitats, the tigers are becoming threatened in India. Large landscapes like Central India holds great promise for this, if Project Tiger (now National Tiger Conservation Authority) can succeed in its efforts to establish a large uninterrupted landscape including Kanha Tiger Reserve. Perhaps this will be the best tiger landscape in the world. Every one's cooperation and whole hearted support is required to make this venture a success.

————————·••••••·————————

4

GIFTS FOR A PRESIDENT

Flood lights flooded the cargo holding hall of Singapore Airlines in Changi International Airport in Singapore, as photographers focused their lens on the crates holding two white tigers, handled for the first time by the staff of the airline. This was much to the annoyance of the young white tigers, who did not know as to where they are going or why they have been lodged in these crates shifted from their spacious open air enclosures of Nandankanan Zoological Park and being shifted from place to place.

The story perhaps dates back to few hundred years, when Orissa (now Odisha), then known as 'Kalinga' was basking in its glory of a great maritime empire. Odia businessmen, known as 'Sadhabas' used to trade with far off islands in the Indian Ocean like Java, Bali, Sumatra and Borneo, now parts of Indonesia. The Sadhabas used to launch their sailboats called 'Boitas' on the Kartika Poornima day, the full moon day in the Odia month of Kartika, coinciding with English months of October/November taking advantage of favourable wind and sea currents. As the rivers were rather deep, their ships could start from Cuttack lying 90kms inlands and other nearby places. As the centuries passed by, perhaps the sailboats lost their ground and gave way to steam and then diesel powered ships. The river mouths also started getting silted up, preventing navigation of large vessels through them. Of course, steamships continued to operate from large number of smaller ports of Orissa Coast like, Balasore, Chandbali, Dhamra, Ganjam and perhaps Gopalpur. Even trade with Burma (now Myanmar) continued through the sea route from these ports. As a child, in early fifties of last century; in 1951, I had my first glimpse of a ship in Chandbali berthed there to take a load of rice to Burma.

The old maritime tradition of starting the voyage on the *Kartik Poornima* day has since stopped. But it has not yet been forgotten. It is still alive in the form of a ritual of sailing lighted banana-stem boats with oil lamps in rivers, lakes and other water bodies in early mornings of that day by Odias to commemorate this age old Kalinga tradition. This is celebrated through a weeklong festival at Cuttack called *'Bali Jatra'* as Bali island of Indonesia was perhaps the most favoured destination of *Odias*. This is also celebrated as *'Boita Bandana'* in Paradeep port every year.

Incidentally, almost half a century back flying to Indonesia, then in Dutch occupation, a young daring Odia pilot Bijayananda Patnaik, popularly known as Biju Patnaik could rescue Dr Sjarhir, the electedPrime Minister of that country, while the Dutch force was all around. He airlifted him in his small Dakota aircraft without any concern for his personal safety. This heroic act was recognized and he was awarded the highest civilian award of that country *"Bhumiputra"* much later, after Indonesia's independence. This was one of most daring rescue venture in history. He became a very good friend of President Sukarno. This young man became popularly known as Biju Patnaik in later years and he became the Chief Minister of Orissa twice.

During his second term in office as the Chief Minister, he hit upon an idea of reenacting the traditional '*boita*' sailing to Bali from Paradeep port following the route followed by *Sadhabas* as ascertained from the sketchy descriptions available. He also wanted to bring both the countries India and Indonesia closer through cultural exchanges.

A sailboat was constructed and a naval crew was put together to perform the long journey with an Odia girl selected to join the team after a search process. It was also decided to take few performing artists and craftsmen with handicrafts for a 'festival of Odisha' there. Two ministers and number of state officers also accompanied Sri Biju Patnaik to Indonesia in order to showcase Odisha.

It perhaps struck to him that; Odisha is a state that is proud of her white tigers bred in Nandankanan zoological park. He wanted to present a pair to President Suhaorto as a gesture of good will. A massage was sent from the Ministry of Environment and Forests of India indicating that these are gifts to the children of Indonesia from the children of India. Out of about 25 white tigers a search was made to locate the most ideal ones. It was decided to take two young animals nearly one year in age, so that they can stay in Indonesia for longtime and breed. They should be of different parents to prevent inbreeding as far as possible. Breeding of animals using closely related animals leads to inbreeding depression, which often causes deformities among the progeny and makes them susceptible to diseases. Though white tigers were bred in Rewa in Central India for the first time; Nandankanan accidentally got three white tigers cubs from a tawny pair not known to have any relation with the Rewa genetic line. White tiger Diana of Rewa lineage was also brought from Delhi Zoo and renamed Subhra. She was also mated with the white tigers of Nandankanan. Thus 3 lines of white tigers – Nandankanan, Nandankan -Rewa and pure Rewa origin were housed in the park making it really unique collection of white tigers. Even a white tiger-breeding project was supported in the park by the union government in early eighties.

The male white tiger Ajaya. Photographed by K. L. Purohit

The female white tiger Malati. Photographed by K. L. Purohit

Fifteen months old Ajay born to parents Anand and Krutika and Nine months old Malati parented by Pinaki and Bishakha were picked up for the air journey abroad. Ofsprings of different parentage were deliberately picked up to prevent inbreeding, which is detrimental to their progeny. Though they were young animals, they looked like adults and were in excellent health. Crates were made as per the specification given in the export guidelines for air transport for animals and they were fed well or rather overfed with choicest soft pieces of meat to see them through the transit, as it is quite well known that they will refuse any food during transit, because of the confinement, travel, stress and noise etc; a very strange experience for them. They were given food in their feeding cubicles and then coxed in to the transport cages, where two new stainless steel pots were tied with thick wire and filled with water mixed with glucose. There was opening for topping up of water and provide food whenever necessary. I had to accompany the animals as the park Director with Sri Kamal Purohit, the then Range Officer who looked after the animals, as the journey was to be performed in three phases. The journey from Bhubaneswar to Calcutta airport was to be performed by road. From Calcutta to Singapore and then to Jakarta was to be traveled by air in two spells. It was not known yet if any further journey shall be involved for these young felines as that were to be decided by the Indonesian Govt.

We started from the park. As usual the park staffs were very sad to leave them to go to another far away country. Particularly some of staff that cared for them as cubs and were not accompanying them to Calcutta broke down when they lifted the crates to the truck. A unique man animal relationship or bond that is difficult to appreciate unless experienced.

Air-India was to carry us along with the felines to Singapore from where we had to fly to Jakarta in a Singapore Airlines flight after an overnight stop over.

As our Boeing 747 touched down at Changi International Airport in the evening 0f 1st, February, 1993 and slowly taxied to get attached to one of hundred and odd chutes of the terminal of one of the two terminal buildings, the cabin intercom announced a welcome to us by name, indicating that a lady is waiting for us outside the chute. Oh there she was, a sari clad lady of Chinese descent waiting with a small floral bouquet and a massage from Vijay Kumar, Curator of Singapore Zoological Park, who was waiting for us somewhere in the terminal. After we completed our arrival formalities and descended to the arrival lounge, there was Mr. Kumar waiting to take us to the cargo area of the airlines more than 10 kms away. Our feline friends had already been transferred to the Singapore International Airlines (SIA) for their onward journey to Jakarta. The airline personnel were really thrilled and had contacted the Singapore Zoo to provide all assistance for handling the animals during their overnight stay. Mr. Kumar even got 10 chickens for them. The airline was about to carry their first white tiger cargo in its long history of commercial aviation. It was important for them to document it in celluloid and paper for their publicity. Hence there was a crowd of scribes and photographers.

I knew that these animals shall not accept any food, however tasty it is, as is usual with large cats in transit. They even did not accept the chickens; so much liked by them in normal situation and started growling in range. We requested the SIA staff to give them a little privacy by asking lens men and reporters to move away. As we opened to clean up the crates and provide water, we were surprised to see that new water pots, the only objects in the crates had been mangled to un-recognizable shapes. But water was badly required for maintaining body fluid. We arranged to provide water with glucose to give some energy. SIA staff was confident that they could handle the animals till they are loaded in their flight to Indonesia.

Mr. Kumar took us to the Zoo Guest House for a night's stay in the little tranquil hut, outside the famous zoo close to the Malayasian boarders with Singapore. I have always got the worm hospitality of the zoo when I have touched Singapore as Nandankanan had maintained a long association with the zoo and maintained frequent interaction in technical matters. Of course zoo personnel of the whole world treat themselves as part of a global zoo family.

We were up on the next day early in the morning to prepare for going to the airport to take the flight. Zoo was not yet open. We reached the airport, in a taxi and checked in and reached the departure lounge of our flight. Through the large glazed openings of the lounge, crates of Ajay and Malati waiting to be loaded to the aircraft were clearly visible. Though I could not see them in the morning due to security formalities, I checked up from the SIA staff that they were doing fine. As we were waiting, I saw a forklift truck take the crates one by one to an inclined conveyor belt, which was to take them to the baggage space below the passenger cabin of the Jumbo Jet about 6-8 meters above the ground. The crates slowly moved up till they got inside the baggage hold to be kept in a pressurized compartment earmarked for animals. Here air pressure and temperature are maintained at normal atmospheric pressure and a comfortable temperature of 24^0 Celsius, though the temperature outsides dipped to $(-)$ 30^0Celcius or still lower when the aircraft flies at 10,000 mts. or above.

As we got into the aircraft and watching safety precautions in the television screen, sounds of scratching came at regular intervals from below our floor. Though other passengers might have ignored it, we knew that our large cats are placed immediately below our seats and are making this noise in annoyance, as they had no way to know as to where they are and why their companions of Nandankanan are not seen.

Our flight, after it left Changi airport flew over the Java Sea, briefly flying over Sumatra island of Indonesia before touching down at the Jakarta airport in Java Island. As we cleared the formalities and came out to the arrival lounge, of this beautiful airport with lush green lawns, murals and very pleasing ambience, the 1st Secretary of Indian Embassy introduced himself and took us straight to the cargo bay of the airport. There a small crowd headed by the Minister, Forestry of Indonesia was already waiting with press and electronic media. We transferred the travel, export and health documents of the tigers with the keys of the crates to the Indonesian authority along with the birth details of the animals. I had to answer scores of questions to a very enthusiastic press, interpreted to them in 'Bhasa Indonesia. They were quite happy to receive the gifts. We learnt that a flight is getting ready to airlift them to Surabaya due east of Jakarta in the same Java Island to the 2ⁿᵈ largest Zoo of that country, as decided by their government. It was indeed a sad moment for both of us to part from these two animals; that we may never see again. We ensured that their crates are clean and supplied with food and water. Their new keepers were explained through interpreters about their care as English is not understood by common people of that country.

We were now free to proceed to Bali Island where our Chief Minister and other members of the delegation had already reached. We took an afternoon flight of 'Garuda International Airlines' their national carrier, to Denpasar International Airport the entry point to Bali Island, a tourist destination. We had to advance our watch by 1 hour. I did not know that Indonesia, because of its large spread in the sea, with more them 12000 islands has 3 time zones.

This small island with about 95% of its population being Hindus gets visitors from all over the world. Tourist facilities have been well developed. Its airport, hotels, taxi service, market places, orchid culture, handicraft, beaches and friendly people all have geared up for the tourists.

We checked in to a small hotel and met with other members of the team and discussed about modalities of gifting and attended a dinner arranged in Hotel Bali Oberoi for the Governor of Bali and other dignitaries. Our Chief Minister personally directed the menu, an 'Odia-Balinese Mix' and looked after the guests.

Next day was a Thursday. As we went round Denpasar and neighboring areas and market places, we saw almost all women folk busy making garlands of flowers for offering to the Hindu deity. When the taxi drivers came to know that we are Hindus from India; they warmly greeted us. Though Bali is a predominantly Hindu province, rest of Indonesia is Muslim majority. It is said that the Muslim traders from Gujrat brought Islam in to that country back in the 7th/8th century. Ancient Hindu temples are found all over Indonesia and are well maintained till date. Even Muslims practice Hindu type rituals, dresses and have *Sankritised* names. Their handicrafts depict Rama, Ravana, and Garuda and so on; the mythological characters from Hindu scriptures.

We returned to Jakarta the next morning for presenting the tigers formally to the President. It was to be presentation of the 'Citation' printed on silk and blow up of Ajay and Malati, the white tigers. I met our Chief Minister in his room in Hotel Indonesia close to where I stayed in Hotel Kartika Plaza. He told me that due to security reasons, the time of presentation had not yet been fixed. He advised me not to wait any more and leave all the materials with our Ambassador and go to see places of my interest like zoo, wildlife or other places of tourist interest in a short time available before we start our return journey.

I left the citation and blow ups with our Ambassador as our loving young tigers were already a thousand kilometers away from Jakarta and several thousand kilometers from their place of birth. Perhaps they are establishing friendship with their new companions both men and felines and must be receiving a lot of attention from the people of Surabaya who would have seen white tigers for the first time, in a country which had tigers in large numbers in the last century, but almost lost all of them in the wild. Our last string of thread connecting them to us has been severed and I did not know if I would meet them ever again. I wished them good luck and felt sad for a moment.

During my stay in Jakarta I saw Taman-mini, a theme park developed to expose the tourists to the history, geography, culture and life style of different parts of the country. Indonesia, a country of many islands, was shown in a large relief on the ground, complete with water stretches, depicting typical houses, gardens etc. in them, which could be seen from a cable car. A large museum depicted different tribes, their costumes and cultures, history of the country, brides and marriage costumes etc. A large theatre with a very large screen presented three-dimensional films for about 15 minutes. It was an excellent introduction to a beautiful country.

We visited an open zoo and amusement park called Taman Safari at Bogor run by Dr. Manansung, whose family owned a large circus that toured different parts of the world. This safari, located in a valley with undulating topography close to tourist town of Bogor, toured by visitors through different open-air exhibits having different species of carnivores as well as herbivores in a protected coach. He has used his skill of managing the circus in this beautiful park and is doing good business, while he has taken up some ex-situ conservation programs of breeding of endangered species, according to modern zoo standards. He has set up an amusement park, hotel and restaurant within the campus also.

A visit to Ragunan Zoo, Jakarta was quite interesting. We had a complete round of the beautiful zoo, set in a well wooded country side like Nandankanan that housed many species peculiar to the region like large number of orangutans, white handed gibbons, false gavials, tapirs and so on.

The Orissa contingent presented an excellent cultural programme that evening in honour of dignitaries of Jakarta and the Indian community.

We left for India the next day through Singapore and Bangkok. The beautiful and professionally managed Singapore Zoo had always been an attraction for me.

But the Dusit Zoo in Bangkok, in the heart of Bangkok city was a sea of humanity on a Sunday morning when we visited the park. To our utter surprise an open-air platform close to the entrance was hosting a 'Cabaret' dance programme accompanied by very loud and hard music kept the audience enthralled. This is in sharp contrast to the Indian Zoo standards, where even children parks, amusement in from of boating, eating houses and display of some domestic animals like mithuns, camels or pigeons are discouraged. Indian Zoos do not allow performing of animals in zoos. Many zoos in Europe and even Singapore Zoo practice different animal shows performed by apes and monkeys like breakfast with orangutans etc. etc. Area wise this Govt. run zoo is a small zoo covering about 16Ha had a water body and housed large number of species bought from different parts of the world. Most animals were kept in open moated exhibits. But commercial emphasis to the zoo management weighed heavy against the conservation angle. We met Dr. Usum, the Director General of Zoos in Thailand. Dr. Ususm had his education in Mussoorie in the Himalayas and spoke English well and is a well-known figure among ASEAN zoos.

Bangkok to Calcutta was our last hop back to India after presenting our white tigers to the President of Indonesia, was not quite eventful.

———————————— ·✦✦✦✦·· ————————————

MAN EATING LEOPARDS OF JEYPORE

It was a winter morning, when I with my colleague Sri Sudhakar Mohapatra, then Conservator of Forests of Berhampur Circle, who was also looking after Koraput circle were descending down the slope of, meandering *ghat* road from Koraput on our way to Jeypore. I was invited by Sudharkar Babu to identify a carnivore which had killed seven persons and injured several others, besides attacking goats and other live stock within 8 km radius of a very sparsely forested area of Koraput circle. This spot was located not far from Jeypore town on the road to Boipariguda. The people of the area were agitated and had even threatened to boycott the approaching assembly elections en-masse, if this menace is not stopped and any further casualties prevented. I was told that one old man was taken from a fire place where people slept after a religious programme, *Astaprahari,* the previous night. He was taken one and a half kilometers from that place up a fairly steep hill and almost the entire body was devoured by next afternoon. It was not tiger country, as there was no forest worth the name except small bushes, badly hacked by people. Of course such undulated topography with bushy vegetation is a good habitat for leopards. But wild prey base was almost absent. Besides, how can a leopard devour entire body of an adult person and even drag it such a distance up a fairly steep slope. I thought for a moment that it could be an old or injured tiger that cannot stalk a fast prey, had turned in to a man eater. But a tiger cannot be going so stealthily and if he was operating in that area for more than a month, he could not hide himself in such short bushes, of which almost every inch is visited by cow herds, fuel wood gatherers and others every day. Even it did not stand to logic that an injured or old tiger could carry a full grown person such a distance up the slope. It was essential to locate a few pug marks. Though the pugmarks of tiger and leopards are identical, the pugmark of an adult tiger is far larger than that of a leopard. Normally a pugmark of a tiger cub is confused with that of a leopard. In a census operation they are differentiated by measuring the length of the stride, a distance between front and hind pug marks. This distance is much longer in case of an adult leopard. But the ground was so hard that there were no pug impressions. On the ground some drag mark was visible. As we were analyzing more and more different information, the topography of the area and vegetation, more mysterious it was appearing. A camp had already been set up by the staff drawn from different areas of the Division and mobile staff, who had also managed to make a wooden box type trap, like a trap for rats.

We decided to visit other villages, where the animal had recently attacked. No one appeared to have seen the killer.

Was it a wolf? Wolves are known to be stealthy child lifters, when they need lot of food to keep their young ones properly fed. This has happened in the past in Athagarh and Angul areas and in many parts of Northern India where wolves wrecked havoc by lifting large number of children and babies, without being noticed. This was a perfect habitat for wolves. But it is impossible for a wolf to lift a full grown man.

In another village a man was lifted from among the family members, who slept outside the house near a fire place. Not far from there another person was injured on the neck, and when people shouted in panic the animal fled in to the darkness. Nearby, the wooden door of a goat pen was pushed and the wall scratched. It was here, I could make up my mind that it was a leopard, as a tiger could have easily pushed down the flimsy door and would not have made scratches like that.

If it was a leopard, it cannot be single one. It was definitely a team of more than one, which was working as a team. Were they a male of female team? It was not very likely, as these large cats seldom lived together except during mating. I had no way to establish this in the absence of any clear pug mark. The female pugmark is rectangular, while that of the male is squarish.

But the cubs remain with the mother till they can hunt independently; this continues almost up to one and half years. From all indications, I was convinced that it is a mother and sub adult cub or cubs' team which is causing this havoc. Sudhakar Babu, who was a very seasoned wildlife officer and was former Field Director of the Similipal Tiger Project, agreed with me almost completely.

We consulted the topographical maps of the entire area, noted the places where the team had recorded cases of attacks, either of men, cattle or dogs. One village close to a forest area had suffered the maximum damage among all the villages. The attack on people was restricted to sleeping people, which indicated convincingly that the mother has suffered some injury, for which she is unable to stalk a moving prey, however slow. But both of them are sharing the load to carry the prey. Leopards have quite strong jaws, very powerful for lifting or dragging a prey. Even it has been observed that they can carry young *cheetals* held in their jaws and climb up trees.

The man being dragged up the hill.

After analyzing the topographical maps of the entire area and discussing with the Forest staff on the spot, it was decided to attempt trapping the animals, as it was very difficult to tranquilize them. The leopard is a very cunning animal and famous *shikaris* have found it extremely difficult and time consuming to shoot down man eating leopards in comparison to the tigers.

The mother leopard being trapped.

I decided to set the trap not far from the place, where the goat pen was attacked, under a Mohwa *(Madhuka Letifolia)* tree and provide a goat as bait. When the animal dashes against the wall between the trap chamber and the bait, the drop gate would fall, trapping the animal or animals. I tested the trap several times and advised to cover the trap with freshly cut brush wood every day and put fresh goat droppings and spray goat urine daily to serve as camouflage to the trap and to send a strong odour floating through the air (olfactory signal) to lure the animals. Though leopards have good vision, their sense of smell is stronger.

The staff did not appear quite satisfied, as they did not seem to visualize the end of their ordeal of staying in cramped tents far away from their families. We explained to them our logic and advised them to keep the people away from the vicinity of the trap area and maintain silence and do not use torches at night. They were asked to report daily developments. We returned back, Sri Mohapatra came to Berhampur and I came back to Bhubaneswar, where I was to look after Nandankanan the famous zoological park as its director.

I kept telephonic contact from Bhubaneshwar, 550 kms away from the designated spot. Days passed by. By fifth day the staff appeared to be disappointed. But they reported that a leopard did visit the area. I asked them to keep on changing the brush wood and putting fresh goat dung and urine. On the eighth day my telephone rang. It was the D.F.O., Jeypore on line. He was jubilant that a female leopard had been trapped. I advised him not to remove the trap as the sub adult cub shall definitely come there. I dispatched a truck with two cages and the veterinarian to get them to Nandankanan.

Dr. Patro, the vet proceeded to the spot and transferred the female leopard in to the cage and sought my permission to return back. The people were quite jubilant and mood of local staff was quite upbeat. They had forgotten all their ordeal of staying in the tents for a long time. Instead, I asked Dr Patro to wait and tell me if the leopard had any injury. After a close examination, he informed that she had one finger on the left fore paw cut. My suspicion was confirmed that this had resulted in making her stay close to habitation and prey on slow or sleeping animals.

Three more days of waiting followed, when one night, the goat started bleating nonstop. The staff rushed to find a young male leopard in the trap. He was a sub adult animal, in perfect health and had acquired trait of man eating from the mother. Had he not been trapped he could have become a vicious killer for long time and would have passed on the trait to his off springs. This is what happens to tigers too.

Dr Patro, caged him also and brought the mother-son duo to Nandankanan Zoological park which became their home for rest of their lives.

Normally these animals live on wild herbivorous prey, which they stalk and prey upon. But fragmentation of habitat and clearing the forests has resulted in fewer prey populations and thereby increase in conflict with humans and other domestic animals. As a result animals get injured by snaring, arrows and sometimes by country made guns. This makes them incapable of hunting and forces them to prey on cattle and men, which are not their natural prey. This ends only when he or she is eliminated, reducing the small, threatened population of tiger or other large cats further.

The tiger habitat is shrinking quite fast and turning to scrubs more suitable for leopards, due to human onslaught. Thus the tiger number has gone down drastically in Odisha while the leopard population had been rising. Of course, more than half the tiger population is confined to Simlipal Tiger Reserve; thanks to the 'Project Tiger' a very successful programme launched by the central government in 1973.

Let us help in protecting their habitat to see that these large cats survive at least beyond the next century. This will also help our successors on this earth to breathe clean air, drink clean water and see more greens around where they live.

6

THE ESCAPADE

It was a September afternoon in1989. I was on my way to the Nandankanan Zoological Park in my Gypsy, when the radio fixed in my vehicle for communicating with the zoo, came to life and informed me that 'Sudharani' has escaped in to Chandaka sanctuary. The news took me by surprise.

'Sudharani', a young cow elephant brought from Karnataka, a South Indian State where she was caught through pit method of capture as a 6 years old on the 25th, February, 1964. She was kept in Mercara Elephant camp of the state forest Department. The Orissa Forest Department bought her on payment of Rs12,420/- on the 24th, March, 1975 for use in Nandankanan Biological Park for joy rides. She was in Nandankanan for about 5 years. She appeared to have a tendency of escaping, which she exhibited first on the 8th, April,1975, less than a month after her arrival in the park, when she threw her Mahout, Guna Khamari from her back while moving for exercising. Again on her way to Satkosia for using her for patrolling in April, 1987 she disobeyed her keepers and escaped near Jatamundia, after moving about 20 Km, perhaps hearing the noise of a rice milling machine and injured few cattle and damaged some houses. But, he could be re-captured at Dompada with the help of other cow elephants named Radharani and Prema. As a last effort she was transferred to the camp near Chandaka Wildlife Sanctuary with her Mahout for her better up keep, due to availability of good fodder there and to be used in patrolling work and later for tourism in the sanctuary.

Chandaka was a forest patch of nearly 200 Km^2 close to the State Capital of Bhubaneswar. It was earlier a fairly rich forest with good population of tropical wildlife, particularly elephant. When the state capital shifted from Cuttack to Bhubaneswar, excessive biotic pressures from the migrant population reduced the forest to a scrub forest mostly covered with *Eupatorium,* a weed, termed also as an alien invasive species. But about 60 elephants continued to stay there and cause havoc to the life and properly of the people in the populated area around the sanctuary. This conflict resulted in death of few elephants and few people every year. Some elephants became too aggressive due to injury caused by burring wood thrown at them, by arrows or pellets of country made guns when they chased and attacked people with slightest provocation. Many of them had to be declared 'dangerous to human life' under the Wildlife (Protection) Act, 1972 by the Chief Wildlife Warden and eliminated. Though men are to blame for the entire sequence of events, elephants had to pay the price. The State Govt. decided to preserve this patch of forest and a scheme was prepared by a wildlife trained officer

Sri Suresh Kumar Mishra under the guidance of Sri Saroj Ray Choudhury. It was decided to trench this forest and call it an 'Elephant Reserve' and to give its vegetation the protection it needed. These steps paid rich dividends and the vegetation rejuvenated, with Kanta Bamboo clumps and other edible plant species; the principal diet of elephants established everywhere. Water bodies were created. Though the trench could not be completed due to various reasons, the partial protection, provided lot of food materials for the elephants, though the area of less than 200 Km^2 was too small for so many elephants, besides other live stock of villages within the sanctuary. This resulted in drastic reduction in man-elephant conflict and consequent death of elephants and people to hardly any.

Sudharani was brought from Nandankanan to Chandaka to strengthen the protection machinery there. She was kept under a newly built shed at Godibadi, which was the main entrance to the park.

I rushed to Godibadi to see what has happened, as I knew that a tame elephant, when let loose quite often becomes more dangerous as she had lost all fear for man. There was a small gathering of forest staff and the mahout and his assistant. A small group of people from the nearby villages had also gathered to hear the story. The shed was empty. Her mahaut was gathering his few belongings and equipments used for Sudharani while sobbing. On my arrival, the crowd widened the circle and made an opening for me to reach the Mahaut, who stood up and wept. I consoled him and asked him to narrate the story.

Sudharani abandoned the mahaut and escaping into the wild.

At around ten in the morning, as usual he took Sudharani for a bath in a nearby stream flowing from the reserve. There was about one and a half meter deep water in a shallow pool, where Sudharani had sat down, with her mahaut sitting on her. The mate, assistant to the Mahaut was scrubbing her with coconut husk and brick to clean her skin crevices and folds. This is necessary to remove the dirt from the skin folds of elephants and to remove lice and other insects sticking there. Elephants do enjoy this and this operation strengthens the bond between elephants and mahauts. Suddenly a large herd of wild elephants appeared on the other side of the fence at some distance. Because of the dense forest growth it was not possible for Sudharani to see the herd as elephants' vision was not quite sharp, but sense of smell was quite strong. She stopped movement of her ears and raised her trunk perhaps to get some small and sound. But the air was still. She must have got to know about the presence of the herd from their ultrasonic sound, which elephants use to communicate between themselves over long distances, though it is not audible to human ears. Though no research has been undertaken about such communication among Asian elephants (*Elephas maximus*), this has been proved in case of African elephants (*Loxodanta africana*). She got up in a jerk with Roshan still sitting on her and started moving towards the gate. Roshan could not know why, though he could sense the presence of the herd on the other side, though an elephant proof barrier meant to allow water flow only separated them. The slow walk, with water dripping from her body, changed to a canter and them to a run. Roshan was scared and jumped from her back, as no amount of command and use of 'ankush', a sharp instrument meant to control elephants, could stop her. She ran at a speed of about 25 Km/hour and ran crossing the drop bridge over the elephant proof trench to the proximity of the herd. The bamboo brakes obliterated the view of both Sudharani and the herd. They could not see what happened there after.

I analyzed the cause. She was perhaps in estrus, which do occur particularly in winter months in adult females and perhaps a tusker in the herd was in *musth* at that time. This attracted the female towards the tusker. '*Musth*' is a stage of sexual excitement which occurs in adult males both tuskers and *makhnas* (tusk less males) above 15 years of age, usually during winter months. At that time, a fluid exudes from 2 glands on their temple and they behave abnormally and tend to attack people. In case of captive ones, the mahauts are most vulnerable. In many cases they have killed the mahauts. This stage continues for up to 3 weeks. When this is detected, they are tied up, given only grasses and water and sprayed frequently. There are many *ayurvedic* (traditional Indian medications) medicines which are also applied to shorten the period of *'musth'* in tame elephants. Different medicines are used in different areas, as India has a very long history of war elephants. Even now large numbers of tuskers are kept in temples of South India and Sri Lanka for religious processions. Guruvayur temple in Kerala near Thrissur has a very large herd. Sometimes tranquilizing drugs are used to control them.

We were worried about Sudharani and Roshan was weeping. She still had a rope around her neck and a steel chain tied to her right fore-leg for tying her in the shed. I instructed our staff, particularly Banshi, 'the elephant tracker' to keep a watch over Sudharani and asked Roshan to see if she responds to his call.

Over the next month or so she was seen with the herd several times. Twice or thrice Roshan called her out from a distance. She raised her trunk in acknowledgement. But two other adult females crossed their trunk in a gesture asking her not to go away.

I thought of immobilizing her and capturing her when she is seen nearby. Banshi informed one day that she is about 5 Kms away from Godibadi. I went with the staff and Dr. Acharjyo, a very experienced and well known veterinarian of the country, who was associated with Nandankanan from its very creation in 1960. It was December, 11 and the herd was grazing in a thicket of bamboo about 30 m. from a forest road. I knew that tranquilizing her will be risky while other elephants are around her. After she drops down after tranquillization, others may not move away from the site and make recovery impossible. But, I loaded the tranquilizing gun with the drug and a rifle for safely. Dr. Acharjyo, the D.F.O., Banshi and I tip toed through the bamboos, bending, sitting or crawling, in order not to alarm the herd. The wind direction was also favorable and I was sure that they shall not be getting our small. We inched forward. As we moved about 5 to 6 meters though the thicket, the dry bamboos under our feet broke making some noise accompanied by the crushing noise of dry leaves, though we maintained silence and visual contact. The entire herd of about 20 elephants with 2 tuskers, cow elephants and calves slowly moved closer. Sudharani was almost in the middle trying to spot us. As we further moved, one older female made a sound ket….. ket….. ket….. I knew this is an alarm call for the herd. They have several sounds, with different meanings for them.

I thought it will be too risky to proceed further. It was more risky because we in Orissa had to tranquilize elephants on foot, as we did not have trained 'Kunki' elephants for the purpose. In all other states chemical immobilization through dart gun, a sort of two stage rocket was done from elephant back, eliminating the risk of an attack in case of failure to tranquilize. Sudharani was in good health and appeared to enjoy the new found company, two thousand kilometers from her place of birth in Nagarhole in Karnataka. We decided to leave her alone. Our staff saw her at intervals during their normal tours. I am told that she has already given birth to more than 2 calves after 18 months of gestation and is quite a good mother. She was enjoying her freedom.

Her safety with that of her young ones and other wild animals is dependent on the protection of Chandka, from the biotic pressures from surrounding villages and expanding Bhubaneswar city.

After almost two decades of the incident, though the vegetation of Chandka has improved due to better protection and status of other species has improved, almost all elephants have left the reserve and gone south towards Ganjam in several herds and are in no mood to return. Many of them have died due to train accident, electrocution and other causes as the surrounding area has since been highly urbanized with many institutions, high rise structures and lighting with no viable corridor that connects this forest to other forest patches, left for their return. But Chandka in close proximity of the capital city need all protection to sustain other wildlife, while helping in recharge of ground water and for serving as a carbon sink for the ever increasing atmospheric pollution generated due to burning of fossil fuels in various forms in the twin-city of Cuttack and Bhubaneshwar.

----------- ·•••••· -----------

7

ELEPHANTS OF THOLKABAD

It was a winter afternoon of December, 1963. My bus carrying me and my other Khaki clad colleagues rolled, from Chaibasa, meandering through the luxuriant stretch of Sal forest of Saranda in Singhbhum district of Bihar (now Jharkhand state) reached Tholkabad, the site for our camp for next three days. The deep red soil supported a very rich Sal forest, some of the best in the country. This red soil generated clouds of red dust that covered our dresses and body including head to be cleaned painstakingly with buckets of water after we reached the camping site. We were enjoying the sylvan surrounding of Sal, Asan, Bija, Rai, Gambhar, and Haldu, oblivious of the red dust. We had eaten our packed lunch of *parathas*, dry curry, boiled eggs, pickles and bananas which we carried in small lunch boxes kept in haversacks.

While travelling in old fashioned buses the cool winter breeze was blowing through the open windows of the bus. This was usual time for field botany exercise. Some who were strong in botany were asking the weaker ones to identify different plants. Our failures filled the bus with loud laughter. It was the East India Tour for the trainees of Indian forest College, Dehradun of which I was a participant.

The bus crossed several kilometers of forest stretch; small tribal villages of mostly with huts neatly painted with red, white, yellow and black soil and decorated with beautiful tribal paintings surrounded by barren agricultural fields, lying bare after the monsoon crop harvest. Low hills were seen rising from small villages and hamlets. This tract was part of Chhotangpur plateau.

Slowly the bus entered a large saucer shaped valley with a small hillock, with a white bungalow on its top. The house on the plateau was the Forest Rest House, used generally by the senior forest officials of the states on tour. British foresters constructed a large network of rest houses in deep forests throughout the country to facilitate forest inspection. Their sites used to be very carefully selected to provide excellent view of the sylvan surroundings not far from natural water sources. Till the first half of last century foresters used to tour usually on foot, on horses or on elephant back. Sometimes bicycles were also used as means of transport. Jeeps made their appearance in forest gradually after the Second World War.

A flat area was cleared below the hillock for our camping in tents. It was a breath taking view. We all started pitching our tents in two neat rows facing each other and the kitchen and dining tents were pitched on one end of both the rows forming a 'U' shape. We hurried with fixing and securing the tents before the nightfall. The shadows of trees were lengthening and the shadow of the hill was fast covering the valley from the western side. As the temperature was dipping, the trainees were putting on their pull- over. Our room boys appeared from the mess with kettles of hot tea and 6 cups each for serving them to us near our tents. We were arranged in groups of six in each house, which had one room boy each. It was indeed a very refreshing luxury after a long and tiring journey through rough forest road. Fire was arranged at three places in the opening where the local tribes, who were engaged in cleaning the area, huddled around the fireplaces to keep themselves warm.

Darkness descended over the camping site quite early as night sets in eastern India much earlier than Dehradun. The place became absolutely quiet except for congregation in the tents and kitchen at one end. Of course, the surrounding forest reverberated with call of a sambar stag, call of peacocks from their tree top perch and occasional call of languor all alarmed by our presence in white tents. There was very occasional movement of trucks carrying timber and firewood to Rourkela, the steel city of Odisha, not far away. It was around 7.00 in the evening; not far from our camp a noise came from the north, almost like starting of a bullet motorcycle, then slowing down and stopping, usual alarm calls of elephants followed by trumpeting of a bull elephant. The tribal men were alarmed and told us that the elephant herd has arrived and they are close by. These pachyderms were expressing their surprise and annoyance perhaps because we had pitched white tents on their route. As they are expected to come close to the camp, the local people advised us to keep the fire lit and some of us should take turns to keep awake to watch the movement of the herd.

We ordered for a quick dinner. The herd of elephants was in everybody's mind. More worried were those from northern and western states of Rajasthan, Gujarat, Punjab, Himachal etc., where there are no wild elephants left and those from metropolis like Calcutta, now Kolkata. All the trainees went to bed and we organized small groups of trainees to take turn in keeping vigil. My turn was for two hours from the midnight. We got up and went to the fireplace, looked all around to make sure if the elephants were nearby. Moon had just risen and there was faint light everywhere. I knew that the elephants can be very stealthy and can stand absolutely still without any sound. My scanning did not yield any result. A truck carrying timber rolled down the road and took a turn towards the camp and stopped. The driver and his helper came out of the truck and came straight to the fireplace lit with big Sal logs. They came to warm themselves, as it was quite chilly. They sat with us and talked about the forest, their earning, Rourkela town and many other topics, besides wildlife they have encountered. In the process, we forget to look around.

It is around 1.00 a.m. a trumpet very close by raised us to our feet. The stupefying sound was from near Shyamal's tent. Shyamal Sarkar from Calcutta city used glasses with thick lenses. He shouted *'Ha-a-a-thi'* and looked for his glasses in the dim kerosene lantern light and almost fell from his folding canvas camp cot.

We rushed to his tent. Most of our friends in other tents had got up and rushed to the tent. There was nothing. In the dim moon light, we saw a group of elephants rushing back towards the forest.

Perhaps the herd came to explore about the tents and when they heard the noise they sensed danger and rushed back. As they had young calves, they were perhaps worried about their safely and did not want to confront people.

It revealed, how gentle these mammoth pachyderms were and how they avoided confrontation. Most of the elephant attacks are for self-defense. When they felt that they are likely to be attacked and there is no escape, they take offensive posture and charge. They normally do not stand any obstacles or alien structure on their path. This is why they often uproot white mile posts. Other reasons for their breaking houses are due to storage of rice, grains and country liquor in hutments.

We stayed awake for the night and next morning discussed more about the behaviour of elephants. Though we were quite alert, the herd did not appear on next three days, though the camp continued there. We learnt that this is a migration route of elephants between north-west Orissa and South Bihar, now a part of newly formed state of Jharkhand. The elephants move over long distances for their food, as their individual requirement of food is about 200 kilograms per day and they are quite wasteful. Unless they change places, they would exhaust the entire fodder resource in the area in no time. While migrating, they also help in seed dispersal of different species of plants and consequent regeneration. These migration routes called 'corridors' are being fragmented due to human settlements, roads and railways, irrigation projects, canals, mining, industries and cultivation etc. The 'Project Elephant' launched by Govt. of India in 1994 is trying to redress this besides taking other protective measures to protect elephant habitat and to minimize human elephant conflict. But this needs support from the people. Unless this is addressed, the Asian Elephants of which India has the largest population is bound to face an uncertain future.

———————— ‹‹♦♦♦♦›› ————————

8

TURTLE PATROL

It was a winter night in Bay of Bengal. Time, about midnight and Moon had just set in the western horizon. A thick fog had engulfed our little private trawler, hired for our inspection of the no fishing zone in the marine sanctuary. It was just a little dot in the vast expanse of the Bay of Bengal. The fog, combined with darkness had obscured any sighting of boats. The breakers were lifting the little raft up to two meters and dropping it. One lone incandescent bulb drawing power from a battery was our sole source of lighting besides a flickering old kerosene lantern in the engine room. Twenty fishermen sat, wrapped in sheets on the hind deck, cluttered with machines, chairs, ropes, anchor and so on. Few forest staff in uniform held their loaded guns and revolvers in a nightly vigil. Three more boats, two of them from the neighboring state of West Bengal, much larger than ours' also lay anchored, tied to our boat. We did not know where we were. The only sound except occasional coughing of few crew members and captive fishermen was the pounding of waves against our and other captured boats. All of us were quite hungry and worried, as the land was no where in sight and the only navigational tool was a compass and a rope that gave us approximate depth of water. The little wooden cabin, where one cannot enter without bending, provided space for sitting 4 persons, Mr. Pratap Kishore Patnaik, Mr. Nilamadhab Mishra, two senior forest officers who had recently retired from Govt. Service, the Divisional Forest Officer, Pradeep Karat and me. As I tried to go to the bench in the front of me to get a torch, the boat rolled and I was pushed back to the wooden wall behind me, hit my head on the plank and tears rolled from my eyes because of the pain.

The operation had started on 28th of February1999 morning. The sky was clear. River Hansua was calm, when two of my senior colleagues, the D.F.O and me boarded a small fast patrol boat fitted with an out board engine and headed for the sea. Incidentally the boat was one out of those seized from the LTTE (Liberation Tigers of Tamil Elam), a banned militant outfit operating off Sri Lankan coast by the Indian Customs. We brought them from them for wildlife work on loan. The purpose of visit was to see the efficacy of protection measures taken for Gahirmatha marine sanctuary, 20 km. wide and 70 kms long stretch of sea declared recently as 'Gahiramatha Marine Sanctuary' along the western coast of Bay of Bengal. This was done in order to provide legal protection to the Olive ridley marine turtles in this stretch of sea, where they stay for about 4 months for mating before nesting in Gahiramatha beach. This is one of three largest rookeries of this species in the world. Fortunately all the three sites are located in Odisha Coast and the state forest department was responsible for protection of these reptiles. To our surprise they had not nested in the previous two years, though their death due to fishing related activities was alarming. There was international concern regarding protection of this species. The declaration of the Gahirmatha Marine Sanctuary was a part of the efforts to provide protection to the species in the sea and prevent trawling and gill netting near the shore, where they mate in large numbers.

All the eight species of marine turtles are endangered as per IUCN red data book, which lists all the species in the world which are threatened. The Wildlife (Protection) Act of India has also placed all the sea turtles visiting Indian coast in its Schedule-I, classifying them as endangered. It was believed that this species stayed and foraged in the Pacific Ocean and came for nesting to this coast and hence was called Pacific ridley also. But later observation, tagging and tag recovery from different parts along Bay of Bengal and Sri Lanka and subsequent satellite telemetry led to a conclusion that this population comes from Indian Ocean, though further study is needed for confirmation.

Wildlife organization of Forest Department of Odisha was naturally the agency to provide protection to this species, which also nested in two other locations, namely Debi river mouth in Puri District and Rushikulya river month in Ganjam District in fairly large numbers, though sporadic nesting takes place all along the coast.

The Forest Department takes help from Indian Coast Guards, Fishery Department., Police, Voluntary agencies and Fishing Associations to perform this massive task for which the organization was not adequately equipped.

This visit was to see as to how this joint effort is working in preventing trawling at least in 5 kms wide coastal waters, where the turtle concentration was the maximum. As we got in to the sea and went close to our camp at Aganasi island, on the river mouth, we decided to shift to a hired trawler, which was being used for patrolling and for maintaining contact with Coast Guard ship which operated from Paradeep port in deeper waters as the department did not have a reliable sea-worthy boat for this purpose. We shifted to the trawler. Mr. Patnaik and Mr. Mishra were lauding the efforts of our staff, which they had not seen any time during their long service career. Dr. C. S. Kar, Research Officer, the 2 A.C.F.s of the division Swain and Rath were sitting on the deck along with other staff with some arms for facing any counter attack and walkie talkies for communication with ships, beach stations and other patrolling parties. We had a quick lunch and proceeded north. I checked my watch. It was 1.30 P.M. enough time for us to reach Dharma Fishing Harbour before sunset, so that we can cruise in Dhamara River to reach Dangmal inside Bhitarkanika Wildlife Sanctuary in the estuary of Brahmani and Baitarani rivers around 9.00P.M. Bhitarkanika is the third largest mangrove forest in the Indian mainland after Sunarbans and Gujrat mangroves, though it was the richest. The turtles were seen in good numbers popping up from the deep blue waters either singly or in pairs.

Everything went fine with no fishing boats in view, until three in the afternoon when fairly large boats, looking like mini-ships came to our view, closer to the shore near Ekakula. The staff said they are from West Bengal or Bangladesh as their shapes are distinct. We gave them signal to stop and headed towards them. Two of them moved too fast for us to catch up and fled the scene, while we could make the third one stop at gun point. It was lifting its gill net. We brought its crew to our boat and lifted the net and found turtles. Seized the boat, released the turtles in to the sea and tied it to our boat, putting our crew to man that boat, as otherwise they could go away dragging us along to their base. The boat was much more powerful than ours. A local boat was next to be stopped and seized. It was already dark. We could see some land marks in the dim moon light and lighting from the Dhamara coast. Then a second boat from Namkhana in West Bengal, a trawler came to our view. We could reach the trawler after a chase, when it was moving while lifting the net. It was quite a difficult encounter. We had already apprehended about 20 people and 2 boats. This was larger than the first one and her crew tried to put up some resistance. But, we were armed. That had a salutary effect. We seized the trawler with net or part of it, as the entire net could not be removed from the sea. This process disoriented us completely. We did not know where we were. We roughly knew our position and knew that we had to go due north-east, before we change our direction to the west to go towards the coast. We maintained radio contract with stations on land, but could not get much help. As we headed north we encountered few more local boats. But decided against seizing them, as we already had too much of a problem in our hands. Instead they were scared away. They did not net and sped away from the sanctuary limits obeying us.

We did not knew how far to go before turning west. We slowly cruised on for about 2 hours being guided by a primitive compass, the sole navigational aid in our possession. The coastal stations lit fire to indicate their locations. But we could not see any. The sea beyond the deck, lit partially by a bulb and a kerosene lantern was dark and ominous looking with sound of the breakers crashing against the trawlers was making us feel desolate and frightened. Most of us were hungry and stomachs were churning. The little boat had no toilet but a suspended plank, a meter below the deck served this purpose and it was very scary to use this contrivance in total darkness with vast dark waters of the sea below. As most of us not accustomed to such life, we looked for alternatives, though there was none. We knew there are many land masses in the area and there was likelihood of hitting one at full speed, if we do not know our location. We proceeded slowly with all the arrested crew of other boats. I was apprehensive, that they may create problems for us, as they were more than us in number, have much more powerful boats and are much better acquainted with the sea. Our trawler driver was of no help as he could not tell us our position. I knew that we should not take any step that will endanger all of us. Besides, if the operation misfired with the Chief Wildlife Warden handling it, it would send a very wrong signal for the entire turtle conservation initiative and wildlife conservation initiatives of the state. I advised them to move due west at a very slow speed, while measuring the depth through the string attached to the boat. Suddenly the depth was reduced to 4 m. Which meant, we were approaching a land mass. But which one was that? I asked them to stop, as the moon went down, the star studded clear sky also got engulfed in the fog that descended on us.

I asked our staff to keep a watch over the arrested crew members and give them tea and whatever eatables, we had, as hunger may drive them to violence and it will be impossible for handful of us to control a much larger number, just kept tied to their place at gun point. We had a hungry and sleepless night but for few cups of tea and biscuit. All night the walkie talkie kept on receiving massages but of no particular use. It was long winter night. We kept on looking west to have a glance of the coast line. But nothing came to our view till it was 5.00 a.m., when we had a faint view of a land mass. Our trawler driver identified it as Udabali Island. We were not very far away from Dharma. But we perhaps went 20 kms out in to the sea that night.

We could talk to our department boat 'Boula', which was waiting for us in Dhamra River overnight as she was not designed to come into the sea. But to our dismay we found that the local boat we had seized has slipped out, taking advantage of darkness and her position, hidden behind a large West Bengal trawler. However, it will not be difficult to get her, as we had all its details. We had already seized more than thirty boats by then during the season and kept in a creek near Barunei to facilitate round the clock watch over them. This had reduced the fishing in the sanctuary, which are also an excellent fishing ground and the fishing season coincides with the turtle season.

All of us heaved a sigh of relief after we boarded Boula and handed over the boats and arrested crew to a much stronger contingent of our staff and had welcome cups of hot tea that we deserved. We started our morning chores and slowly cruised along Kalibhajdian river island in Dhamra river, recognized for its rich mangrove diversity and then through an artificial creek called' Khola, meandering though hanging mangrove branches, stilt roots, fallen logs to the accompaniment of varieties of king- fishers, basking estuarine crocodiles, jumping mudskippers and myriads of unique life forms. We reached Dangmal Forest Rest House, inside Bhitarkanika National Park around 10.00am and recalled the harrowing night's experience after a much needed nap.

I was often asked as to why these turtles come all this distance crossing thousands of kilometers of nice beaches to nests here. This was also the question of my senior colleagues. There is no straight answer, as research has not thrown much light into this aspect so far. But, this is certainly a very unique place and stands apart from rest of them in the south.

This stretch of coast has three rivers namely Hansua, Moipura and Dhamra draining in to the sea with a rich mangrove forest of Bhitarkanika as its hinter land. The human settlers are very few in the hinter land. Hence the following factors must have some effect on nesting.

1. Solitude of the beach and relative freedom from predators like wild dogs, jackals and wild boars etc.
2. Availability of food for hatchlings after they hatch, in the form of micro organisms from the mangrove forests.
3. No lighting on the shore, as lighting disorients young hatchlings that go towards land and are killed due to scorching heat of the sun.
4. Moderate temperature of water due to draining of several tidal rivers.

5. Ideal beach condition with proper sized sand grains, right humidity and texture suitable for digging nests.

These factors perhaps help nesting of up to 0.7 million turtles once or twice a year, spread over for about 7 days each.

The efforts of conservation put up bravely by the forest staff day and night was rewarded later that year in the form of nesting of nearly 0.3 million turtles in March. The year 2000 saw the largest 'aribada' of more than 0.7 millions turtles congregating for nesting in 3 off shore islands. The nesting even did not stop during the day. A conservative estimate puts the total number of juveniles hatched at 50 million giving discount for loss due to digging by other mothers, predators and inundation due to waves etc.

For providing effective protection to the species, we may have to provide adequate trained staff equipped with modern tools, arms, ammunitions, sophisticated sea going boats with full support from the Indian Coast Guards, state police, fishery department and district administration besides support from local community.

But lot more work has to be done, with support from people to save not only the olive ridleys, but many more living creatures and their habitat from extinction from the face of this beautiful mother earth.

9

PROTECTIVE MOTHER

The morning sun was yet to appear in the eastern horizon, but the red glow had already painted the sky crimson. The morning mist was yet to clear the surface of the natural water body, an extension of the Kanjia lake of Nandankanan which was full of aquatic vegetation, decayed floating biomass and deep mud. Few of the shops for eatables for tourists near the gate of the zoo had just lit little coal fires in their hearths, spewing thick smoke, to prepare tea for the staff and their own people. Water birds like jacana and moorhen had just started walking with the elegance of an acrobat performing on stretched wire, over the water hyacinth and lily leaves, peering down to find some food.

The famous Nandankanan Zoological Park, set up in a natural surrounding is an undulated topography comprising of tropical forests, hills and valleys, water bodies and swamps all within an area of less than 5 sq. Kms. These natural attributes make it a unique place which was selected in 1960 to become one of the finest zoological parks in the country in later years. While many species of animals like *Cheetals*, Wildboar, Peafowl, Mongoose and Snakes move freely in its confines, most animals in captivity are kept in open moated and undulating enclosures, forming part of the forest patches which has still been kept untouched.

The swamps behind the residence of the Assistant Conservation of Forests, now also designated as Assistant Director are an excellent breeding ground for Whistling Teals, Purple Moorhens and Bronze Winged Jacanas. The local people also go into these swamps for collecting grasses, snails and different leafs of wetland vegetation.

A village woman went into the swamp to collect snails. As she was moving in the swamp in knee deep water, she was surprised to see seven little ducklings on a large leaf floating on the water. There was no adult bird near about. She thought that, perhaps the mother has either abandoned the little ones or has been predated upon by some animal or man. Her mother's heart melted, as she thought that these little ones shall not survive if left alone, as they can neither find food for themselves nor shall have protection from predators like snakes, predator birds etc. She decided to pick them up with care and give them to the A.C.F., who can take care of these little ones with other animals and birds who live in the Zoo. She very gently picked them up one by one, as they could not fly and were watching with wide open eyes as to what she was doing, with shrill cries. With lot of care she put them in her *saree* and walked straight to the house of the A.C.F.

Ajay Kumar Jena, the then A.C.F. saw the little ones, and decided to care for them in his house, as they were too young to be sent to the water bird aviary. He made a little place on his inside verandah in the court yard, safe from predators like cats and dogs and fed them with fine grains. These little ones got settled and accepted food. The thought of their mother did not occur to anyone, as it was presumed that she was no more. The day passed off, giving way to the night. The little ones had nothing else to do other than huddling together for warmth, missing the cover of the wings of their mother for the first time. Of course an incandescent electric bulb and some paddy straw provided by Ajay did provide some warmth.

Perhaps the mother who was out for foraging during the day and came back to the swamp in the evening to find her chicks missing. As they were not very far away, she could have heard their call and made out the direction where they were.

The door of the court yard was closed at night. It was opened next morning for cleaning. That is when she came looking for her chicks walking awkwardly like the ducks into the court yard. Oblivious of the presence of people, she crossed the courtyard on to the verandah and straight came o the place where her chicks were and settled down with them.

Mother teal with the chicks.

Everybody thought that she will go back either taking her young ones or alone. But that was not to be. She stayed with her family in Ajay's house till the young ones grew up to be transferred to the water bird aviary in the zoo. She stayed along with them in the aviary without any effort to go away choosing captivity than freedom. Perhaps she realized that the young ones cannot go back with her when she came first. Thereafter their long stay in captivity perhaps rendered them incapable of facing their harsh wild world and they felt secure in their new environment assured of food and shelter much more secure for her young ones than in the marshes.

This is one case of maternal love and affection among birds not in any way inferior to any human mother. Such acts might be enacted almost daily in myriads of wetlands, forests and hills in the world among hundreds of species. The cases of long distance annual migration of birds are still unsolved mysteries for science. A little Arctic terns fly from North Pole to South Pole and return every year as a part of their annual migration. Where do they get the energy for this long journey? How do they navigate are all questions, science is yet answer satisfactorily. To our own Chilika nearly a million of them of about two hundred species come from different locations. How do they know of this wet land? Chilika is not the only wetland in the Indian sub-continent or elsewhere in the world. There are many natural and manmade ones including Keoladeo-Ghana, Nalsarovar, Woolar lake and Bhitarkanika, which are also Ramsar sites. These famous wetlands and other less known ones need protection from conversion to habitations or industries and from pollutants. Many birds in the country are highly endangered now like the Great Indian Bustard, White Winged Wood Duck, visiting Siberian Crane, and Jordon's Courser. Many others have vanished. Some birds are also threatened. Can we save them? This should bother all conservationists, wet-land managers, foresters and general public. Let us all work to see that all threatened species come back from the threshold of their extinction and make our planet's avifauna richer.

———————— ++++++ ————————

10

TUSKAR OF HARICHANDANPUR

It was the new year of 1996 in Nandankanan Zoological Park, when usually heaviest crowds of visitors converge on Nandankanan and maintaining law and order becomes a problem for the park management. This year was no different. As the Director of this park, I spent the entire day, coordinating between our staff, police, first aid teams, rescue teams, etc., as about thirty thousand visitors came for visiting Nandankanan on that day. These visitors were to be provided drinking water, sanitation was to be ensured, their safety was to be ensured and teasing of animals by visitors and unruly behaviour had to be prevented. Hence all the zoo staff had to work from early morning to late in the evening to ensure that everything passes off smoothly. The staff was served packed food and water, wherever they were on duty, so that they did not leave their assigned places. Mobile parties kept on moving with walkie-talkies and informed the management about problems anywhere. I also bought a new vehicle, a 'Tata Sumo', which was delivered on that day. This was purchased for helping to meet animal emergencies, particularly outside the zoo any where within the state. These emergencies were quite common and zoo officials were required to handle them, as there was no such unit available anywhere else in the state with the state Forest Department.

I returned home, very tired after the day's work almost at 9.00 p.m. Instead of asking how the day went on, my wife Manju asked me to talk to Sri Niranjan Patnaik, a senior cabinet minister of the state, who had telephoned several times during the day from an interior place and left his number with her. He could not contact me at the zoo as the telephone was not in order and mobile phones were not so common those days. I immediately rang back to be surprised at what I heard. He was at Harichandanpur in Keonjhar District. This is a very small town about 50 Kms. from the district headquarters. He told me that while he was visiting this small town, with the Collector and the Superintendent of Police of the district, he has been *gheraoed* (kept confined) by the people, as a wild tusker has come to the town and was standing in the middle of the small bazaar, after breaking a few houses nearby. I wanted to know, as to what the provocation for the elephant was and why he is not moving out. Was he injured? Are there any other elephants nearby? He told me that there was no injury to him, but there is a small group of captive elephants, who have come from Bihar and they are camping in the mango grove of this little town. He wanted me to rush immediately. The mahouts of the captive elephants requested him to call the Director, Nadankanan to handle the problem.

I could broadly figure out the situation. I was almost sure that one of the cow elephants was in oestrus. But I requested them not to disturb the tusker and wait patiently. I promised them to leave Bhubaneswar by 4.00 a.m. as I needed time to gather my equipments and men and I shall be reaching by eight in the morning. I estimated the driving time to be four hours from Bhubaneswar. It was urgent. I had to act fast. The Veterinarian, the Forest Ranger, Forester, Driver all were informed. All the required equipments to handle a wild elephant like the tranquilizing gun, drugs, rifle, sisal rope, chain, u-bolts etc. were gathered, after making a checklist. We hardly slept and left Bhubaneswar at four as promised. It was quite cold and dark. The new vehicle was being put to use for the purpose it had been procured immediately after its purchase the previous day. The road was quite clear, with very few vehicles plying at that hour.

We reached Ghatagaon, from where we were to divert to a district road to reach Harichandanpur, at around half past seven. When we stopped for a cup of tea and something to eat, to our surprise we saw three captive elephants coming from Harichandanpur. We stopped them and asked about the incident. They informed that the tusker has left the place in the early hours today after staying with them for about fifteen hours. Confirming my apprehension one of the *Mahout* informed that one of the cow elephants was in oestrus. They were very scared. I told them that they should not stop anymore and reach Anandpur early, as they have to pass through elephant tract for some more distance. It is quite probable that another tusker may get her smell and confront them.

The Minister, Collector and S.P. also reached Ghatagaon and narrated their part of the story in the nearby PWD bungalow and now felt quite relived.

We did not return and proceeded to the place, where the drama was enacted, to make sure that the tusker does not return back again. We were surrounded by a large crowd, when we went to the mango grove. They showed us the direction from which the tusker came and where he went. The houses destroyed and damaged by the tusker were also shown to us. They were located close to a village pond where the tusker drank water and took a bath. I talked to the senior most of the Mahouts, who was witness to the entire episode.

He told us that the tusker which came out of the forest was following this group for 3 days. On the night of the incident, he came to the mango grove where the elephants were tied, with their Mahouts sleeping nearby. After they tried to chase him away, he moved away some distance and in a feat of rage, attacked four nearby hutments and broke them. After sometime, he perhaps could not control himself further, and came charging, when the local people and mahouts were scared and moved away from the place where the cow elephants were kept tethered to mango trees. They positioned themselves at a safe distance and saw breaking of the chain of the elephant in oestrus and after intimate contact, mated with her. But he did not leave the village even on the next day and stood on the main road and went to the group on the next night too. He left only after being charged with fire torches and sound of drums and crackers etc.

The wild tusker is trying to take away the captive cow elephant.

Though the captive elephants had left, the people had strong apprehension that the tusker may come back. We traced its retreating path from his footprints up to about 5 Kms. and did not see the sight of the tusker and felt assured that he has returned back to where he came from. Then we reached the site where the incident took place in the mango groove. The entire area, particularly where the young female was tied, was presenting a look of a big fight, full of moist dust and mud with numerous foot prints of both the animals, tusk marks on the trees, impression of the knees and legs besides gel like substance falling at many places, with peculiar odor. I knew that, this smell may attract the same tusker or any other in the forest close by. I advised the staff to turn the soil upside down and make a strong solution of phenyl and spray the same in the entire area. The strong odor will mask the small of secretion from the female.

The people appeared to be quite satisfied, but complained of many elephants moving in the nearby forests, which confront people and destroy their crops. I explained to them that making encroachments in the forest has resulted in fragmentation of the elephant habitat, which deprived them of their preferred food. Besides, paddy, *mohula flower*, mangos and jack fruit etc. grown in these areas are quite delicious food for the elephants, which are already facing shortage of food. Besides storage of home brewed liquor (*Handia*) is very common with the tribal of the locality. Its smell also attracts elephants. I explained to them and the local staff as to how to handle elephant depredation and returned back.

On my way back, I saw the group of elephants with their mahouts, moving quite fast. I had a closer look at the animals and found that all of them are rather weak and one was even limping. It is indeed cruel to use these animals for work as it was difficult to coax them to move long distances on black-topped roads starting from Bihar or Varanasi for begging. The owners of these pachyderms lend out the elephants to mahouts who use them for begging from village to village as people due to their religious sentiment attached with elephants give them rice and money. The Mahout and the owner share the money earned in the process. The elephants irrespective of their physical condition or age have to move from village to village on different terrain and not really taken care of. Though there are rules for their registration etc., quite often they are flouted. It is necessary to stop this by creating public awareness in the matter. Rather all such captive animals should be used in forest protection and other forestry operations, tourism and other lighter works by the organized sector or Govt. who should follow definite set of protocol for upkeep of elephants. Some rules already exist for working elephants of Kerala, Tamilnadu or Karnataka.

We have a great responsibility to maintain their habitat and take care of the captive ones in more humane condition. Let us fulfill this. Of course the best option is not to interfere with their threatened habitat and let them live there without fear.

11

SWIM IN MUD

My telephone rang at my Bhubaneswar residence. There was alarm in the voice of Sri Srivastava. Sri S.S.Srivastava was the Field Director of the Similipal Tiger Reserve, the first such reserve to be set up in the state. I sensed that there was something seriously wrong in Similipal or elsewhere in Mayurbhanj district of which he was in charge. Words were just pouring out of the receiver. He said that eight gaurs (Indian bison) have got in to a quagmire near Debasthali meadow and are unable to get out of there. They are monitoring the situation with their very high frequency radio network (VHF). This place is about 70 km. from Baripada, the headquarters of Similipal Tiger Reserve and takes a minimum of 2½ hours to reach though the shortest route.

The Gaur herd being rescued.

I figured out the scene in my mind. Of course I was not aware that there was such a slushy pool near Devasthali, a place in the core area of Tiger Project, where animal activity is quite intense and sighting of wildlife is by far the best. I realized that it would be impossible to reach the place from Bhubaneswar, as the animals must be struggling for life. I had to give them as much advice that occurred to me, if the animals are to be saved. I figured out in my mind different options available to save the animals. I thought of tranquilization. I knew that if tranquilized' they would go down in to the deep mud, suffocate and die. They could not be brought out.

The other option was to go down and put ropes around their neck and pull them out of the quagmire, while the rescue staff stays on hard ground. It was also quite dangerous on two counts; first, the men going in to the quagmire may not be able to come out and suffer the same fate as the gaurs. The second, they many be surrounded by the animals, making it impossible for them to escape. The animals must also be getting dehydrated very fast and fatigued due to prolonged swimming in the thick mud. I also learnt that there were young ones in the herd. We have to act fast.

I advised him not to waste any more time and proceed to the spot, with ropes, planks, bamboos, glucose, saline drip and life saving drugs to meet any emergency. A senior officer and a veterinarian at the spot could take decisions assessing all aspects of the problem. I also advised to carry tranquilizing equipment to sedate any animal if required.

The rescue team proceeded with all emergency equipments without stopping anywhere. They knew that they had to operate from the hard ground and work very fast as the animals had been exhausted due to prolonged struggle in the mud. Hot sun was making the situation worse. They had to act very fast. Their only option was to use planks and ropes to assist them to come up one by one by pulling them out. One animal would be lassoed and pulled up with the rope with the support of a plank and bamboos. But to the surprise of every one, first rescued bull jumped back in to the swamp; as he saw that his companions were inside the pool. Perhaps he felt more secure in the company of his herd than let loose alone despite the precarious condition in which others were. A lesson was learnt. The team become more careful and pulled them one by one after lassoing and obstructed their return back to the pool. They ran in to the opening one by one. But one of them was too fatigued to move and had to be administered glucose -saline to give him the required strength to move. But the calf could not recover and despite all veterinary care breathed its last. The mission was a success considering, we could save seven out of eight. But everyone was very sad to see the calf dying. The vacant look of the dying calf had robbed the sense of achievement of rescuing seven adults with so much of hard work and untiring efforts. The staff had toiled very hard and worked without food and rest, as no time could be lost in these trifling matters, when the goal was to rescue these beautiful bovines from the brink of death. The team has delivered to the best of their ability and needed all praise and acclaim.

Why did such an incident take place? How could this be known at a place like this where human activities are minimal?

A meadow with lush green grasses had been developed in this valley of Debasthali, close to *Bachhuri chara*. In the winter the cold heavy air descend down the valley and cover the entire valley with deep frost. This kills most of the plants. But hardier ones like Sal gets bunt and stems stand everywhere devoid of branches or leaves, dispersed all over. This presents an eerie look. Debasthali is one such valley from where the non edible grasses had been removed and replaced with good edible grasses and artificial saltlicks had been provided to provide a suitable meadow for the herbivores. There is a perennial stream flowing nearby. Hence herbivores like elephants, sambars, gaurs, spotted deer and barking deer visit the meadows. The carnivores like Tiger and Leopard also lurk around the meadow in the bushy forest and look for their chance to ambush an animal. Perhaps this herd was similarly chased by a tiger. They were alarmed and sped away from the tiger in break-neck speed, without bothering about what is on their path. In this process they jumped in to the quagmire one after the other, least knowing that they will get trapped. Fortunately a forester was going from his residence on the forest road nearby on his daily duty. He saw the gaurs running very fast in a row, getting in to a depression and never came out of the same to the other side. He could not figure out as to what has happened and rushed to investigate. He found the entire herd swimming in the slush and rushed to the VHF (wireless) tower at Debasthali and sent the message to "LION" (code name of the office of the Field Director) at Baripada. The operation followed.

Many such incidences do occur in forest areas and particularly in hundreds of protected areas of the country everywhere involving wildlife. Some are reported and some others are either not seen or never reported. But alertness and compassion for the wildlife can save many of them from accidents like this.

12

COMPASSIONATE GAUR

We humans have always boasted that we are the only intelligent, civilized, companionate or social beings in the entire world and other animals do not have these attributes or feeling, except perhaps the apes, who are acknowledged to be our ancestors or their close relatives, the other primates. But this is far from truth. Many animals are endowed with many such attributes, befitting to their habitat and life style etc.

What follows is a true story at Nandankanan Zoological Park, where we had a very large open-air enclosure to keep Mithuns. This animal, a native of Arunachal Pradesh and upper Assam is believed to be a cross between gaurs (Indian bison) and domestic cattle. They look like over size Holstein Breed of cattle and have a built like a gaur, though their body colour is either white or patchy with black and white patches. They are domesticated in Arunachal Pradesh and often used as an item for barter. The dowry in marriages is also settled in mithun number rather than in a form of cash or other movable properties. The native people use them as beef cattle.

Nandankanan had procured 3 mithuns from Arunachal Pradesh and housed them in an open-air moated enclosure. There they had bred to a good herd and even some of them were given to other zoos on exchange or barter. Exchange is normally the usual way of acquiring animals in most Indians Zoos like barter of mithuns in Arunachal. This is done because; procurement of animals by capture from the wild may deplete the wild population. Hence they are bred in different zoos and exchanged for other animals that are bred by other zoos. The Central Zoo Authority, an agency of the Ministry of Environment & Forests of the Central Government, facilitates such exchanges. Of course in later years, keeping Mithuns in zoos was not encouraged as they were domestic animals.

One fine morning we got news that a gaur calf has strayed in to a village near Nayagarh with the herd of cows and is not going back. He had perhaps been abandoned by the gaur herd as he strayed out of the herd and could not find his way back to the group. Request came to us to bring this young calf to Nandankanan for treatment and rearing. We brought him as a skinny little calf, emaciated after being separate from the mother and deprived of mother's milk. He had not yet started taking solids. He was treated and given milk and vitamins, besides other semi solid food. His condition stabilized and he started putting on weight day by day. His glistening body shine reappeared. He grew to a majestic young bull with white stockings like coat above his hooves, wrestler like shoulder muscles and pointed horns. As he was a lone animal, we thought that he would get a good company with the mithun herd, only if they accept him. He may be kept there till he reaches maturity. He was released in to the enclosure under the watchful eyes of two keepers to observe as to how they behave with each other. First few days were crucial. The adult bull mithun needed to be watched as he could attack the young gaur treating him as his rival to get attention from the cows in the herd. But this transition went of well and they accepted him well in their company

They were all being supplied with grams, other grasses and concentrates together everyday and they enjoyed the food supplied in troughs meant for all of them living together.

Like everyday, on the day of incidence grasses were given to them together. It was not noticed by the keeper, that perhaps there were some insects in the grass. A mithun crow was eating with the gaur from the same platform. After eating for about 15 minutes, the mithun started trembling and her hind legs became loose and she started slumping while her head drooped down and saliva flowed. The keeper started running towards the animal and raised an alarm, though he could not do much as she was quite heavy. But the gaur went close to her and supported her from side for not letting her fall. Hearing the alarm raised by the keeper, the staff ran to inform the zoo veterinarian and to call him. The hospital was about half a kilometer away and hence it took considerable time for the Doctor to reach the spot. The gaur found that he was quite helpless to stop her fall as she was slowly sliding. At this juncture he changed his position without any loss of time and put his head under the neck of the mithun. The entire body weight of the hefty animal was supported on the head of the bull between his two horns, while the keepers helped to support the weight of her hind part supported by her limp legs. Though it was quite enormous weight for the head of the young gaur, he did stand his ground till the Doctor and paramedics reached and treated her and she could again slowly raise her head unsupported. This was a long time. But the young gaur did his best not to let his companion fall till suitable treatment could be provided.

The Gaur supporting the yelling Mithun.

This is an example, which clearly indicates that the animal could know that an animal of another species was uneasy and was about to fall. The fall could be fatal too. He perhaps also knew where to support to prevent a fall and then to shift position to have a much firmer hold. He did not mind the strain taken by his head in the process. He also perhaps knew that the people in the park were taking care of them and shall come to her aid if he can prevent a fall till help came.

We have known of incidents in forests, where gaurs or wild buffaloes have even faced tigers and killed them, attacking them in group. We also hear many stories of different animals helping lost or abandoned animals of other entirely different species. Hence, we are definitely making a blunder when we are under estimating the capability of these mute denizens of our forests and wetlands. They can always take care of themselves in their own habitats, if we save these pristine ecosystems and allow wild animals to live with minimum interference by the humans. Our own survival is dependent on survival of these plant and animal life. Let us give them a helping hand.

13

TUSKER OF MEGHASANI

Standing on a big rock higher than all other hillocks I could see, except a small tower four hundred meters from where I stood, I was gazing down to one of the most breath taking views I had ever seen of nature. It was Meghasani peak in Similipal Tiger Reserve on a clear May afternoon. As far as I could see it was thick vegetation of several shades of green, yellow and purple till the horizon. Sal in full bloom, Kusum trees in their purple foliage and myriads of other trees and shrubs in their unique colored foliage had painted the landscape which no artist could reproduce. This contrasted with clear blue sky and horizon. On the far eastern corner it was navy blue and I was told that in still clearer days one can see the Bay of Bengal very clearly. Many colorful birds were hopping from branch to branch and chirping and calling. A peacock was sitting on a tall tree branch and giving out a full throated call that reverberated in the entire valley below. A male languor was calling 'h-o-o-n----h-o-o-n----h-o-o-n' perhaps to scare us or to alert his troop of our presence. Taking advantage of the elevation of this peak both the Tiger Project Management and State Police had set up stations for radio communication there. This station is very important and life line for the park, as often massages sent from different points are received and relayed to others. This is required as many hillocks obstructed direct transmission of massages, which are vital for protection and management of this protected area. It is a very difficult place to live in, as water at this peak is a difficult commodity to have. As such the water is collected manually and carried in buckets from far below from a spring for different uses. All rations are supplied by the two departments by jeeps periodically. Malaria is common and those living here and other parts of Similipal have to be under regular quinine cover. Still they are not completely immune to it and have periodic bouts of high fever. Unless they are picked up by the departmental vehicle, they have to walk down to the nearest inhabited village, Upper Barakamuda, through most isolated tract, dodging elephants, gaurs, tigers or leopards. That perhaps is the life in most of our protected areas, where the staff brave these odds everyday and continue to guard the wilderness. Hats off to them! Those posted in the urban areas in the state avoid any posting in these inhospitable areas, which result in large scale vacancies, there by further increasing work pressure on very few staff, often quite old and emaciated due to malaria and other ailments.

None of them can keep their families in any of these stations, as neither there are any educational facilities, shopping facility, health services or social life.

I had a long chat with the staff there and advised the Field Director to ease their life to some extent by improving facilities there. We also talked about the four elephants we met on a hair-pin bend while coming up the slope. This group of elephants, who were going down the slope, perhaps to the meadow to graze and take salty soil from the artificial salt lick, made for them by the park management or to take water from the hill streams. Usually all elephant herds rest in shady places during the hot hours of the day and start foraging in the late afternoon. This is also a necessity as being black their skin absorbs heat, which cannot be tolerated by them. Between then till the late morning, before sun gets hot again they travel long distances, depending on the food availability. This is also necessary as each of them need about two quintals of greens per day, of which some quantity is also wasted. If they stay in one area, they will destroy the area completely and make it incapable of regeneration again. It was one of such trip of this small adult herd, when they stumbled across our two jeeps to their surprise. They stopped trumpeted and turned back to take a detour to avoid further contact with us. This is the usual herd behaviour, particularly in Similipal, where they are not harmed by anyone. They have no need for any attack unnecessarily. They avoid any confrontation. We waited there for few minutes and when we found them taking a different route, we went up the slope to reach Meghasani. Perhaps the field staff almost daily meets such herds when they tour in Similipal even on foot.

After some discussion and taking tea offered by the staff stationed there, we walked back to our jeeps slowly studying the flora there and got into respective vehicles. Sun had set and there was a light drizzle. My jeep, petrol driven 'gypsy' was in the front. Light started fading as we descended down, the steep slope. After the steep section of about five kilometers, we came across somewhat gentle slope. As we were coming down still talking about the improvements to be made to the V.H.F. station at Meghasani, suddenly a huge tusker was found rushing towards us. We applied brake and come to a halt. He also stopped. But he refused to budge. He started taking dust from the road and spraying on his body. This is called 'dust bath' for keeping the insects away. Sometimes this is done to keep the body cool. But in a situation like this, this perhaps meant defiance. We proceeded few meters towards him to scare him. But he was not prepared to budge. Even he raised his trunk, removed earth from the ground with his foreleg. We focused our head lights on him. Instead of going back, he stood his ground and even advanced a few steps towards us.

We kept talking between the jeeps with our VHF radios, as almost half an hour had passed in the process. This communication was heard by Meghasani station and through them to all in the park and a discussion as to what is to be done followed. I told them not to talk anymore and create panic everywhere. As nothing happened we decided to bring the diesel jeep to the front, as it is noisier and the noise may scare him. The diesel jeep driver was also quite daring. He crossed us with head lights on and went few meters further. This worked. The tusker that had already picked up a broken branch, perhaps to throw at us started a backward movement with the branch. He went about 10 meters and then stopped. We did not know, whether he was making way for us. He was in the middle of this narrow road. We further proceeded towards him. After some reluctance, he retreated further and stood near a large wild mango tree. We inched forward towards him. He saw that we were stubbornly advancing towards him. He walked to his right and hid his head behind the tree, leaving enough space for us to pass. I knew that he has abandoned his defiant posture and was willing to allow us to go. In this process, he also might be losing precious forging time. In the light we wanted to see if there was fluid flowing from his temple indicating *'musth'* a period of sexual excitement, when elephants behave abnormally and often attack. We could not exactly see, though I thought that it could be the end of a *'musth'* period.

I asked the other vehicle, which had gone back to come together, and speed, with my jeep, ahead without keeping much gap between the two. I said so as I apprehended that the elephant may give a chase, and get in-between both the jeeps, if there was enough gap. We sped away and true to my suspicion, he followed the rear jeep for about 100 meters.

We took almost an hour to get out of the spot. This was an encounter with one of more than 400 elephants that live in this 2750 sq.km tiger project. They have enough fodder, water and cover to live here happily. Even about 100 elephants do come here from Dalma sanctuary of Jharkhand state through Midnapur district of West Bengal. All of them return after few weeks. This an annual phenomenon and they do so as the ripening paddy crop in the vast coastal plains of Midnapur and Baleshwar provides them enough concentrates and allows the Dalma forest a recovery time. I was told that very few individuals stay back in that sanctuary during that period. Their moving together in one very large herd gives them security as they are usually accompanied by few young ones. This herd maintains respectable distance from the resident herds throughout the period of their stay in Similipal foot hills. They can be easily identified by the staff and local people. The elephants turn killers only when they are attacked and injured or unnecessarily harassed when they are foraging. The best way to keep the elephants away from humans and let them live happily is not to harass them and maintain safe distance from them. Asian elephants are getting more and mere threatened due to loss of proper habitat, human-elephant conflict, electrocution and poaching for their tusks. Let us extend our helping hand for their survival.

14

BLACK BUCKS OF GANJAM

It was a vast expanse of green paddy fields interspersed with trees, thatched houses and village roads. After the rainy season, the sky was clear of dust particles, the afternoon sun scattered its golden rays on the paddy fields giving it a gold-green hue. This spectacle against the back drop of deep blue sky of September heightened the beauty of the landscape. As I slowly proceeded towards north towards Buguda, a herd of black looking animals, resembling goats moved in a single file on a field bund to my left. I wondered how so many goats are moving inside paddy fields. My driver – Sanyasi told me that they are *'Kala Bautia'* I did not know what he meant but I became curious and asked to stop. I got down and looked at them closely. To my surprise, they were a herd of seven black bucks with shining black coats, white underbelly, with screw like horns, followed by few light brown coloured does at some distance. These bucks were looking more graceful with their coat tuning extra back at this part of the year after the rains.

Though I learnt about the presence of black bucks in this area, I never had any idea as to how they can live in these isolated pockets in open cultivated land and how they are tolerated by the locals, though they definitely foraged upon their agricultural fields, though agriculture was the main avocation of the people of the area. I was relatively new to the Ghumsur South Division, where I had joined as Divisional Forest Officer. I wanted to know more about them, their distribution, number, food, man-animal conflict, poaching and all other aspects of this species, as not much work was done on the species in Orissa.

My enquiry took me to a finding that the species does not occur only here in the State. They are distributed in the Puri and Ganjam Districts in few patches separated from each other. They were seen in Balukhand in Casurina plantations of Puri Division (now a Sanctuary), coastal Casurina forests of Prayagi, Krishnagiri near Kodala, Kabisurya nagar, Bhetanoi near Aska and Balipadar, Ramanda near Buguda and Karsing in Ganjam District. Though they occurred in so many patches, there concentration is highest near Bhetanoi and Ramanda.

I was curious about these two groups and wanted to know more about them. I talked to old people of these villages. I gathered that they respect this species and believe that, their prosperity depends on their existence. Its history dates back to more than a century, when the villages suffered from a 7 year long famine. Many people died. Perhaps this was the infamous *'Naanka'* famine of mid nineteenth century. Almost at the end of the dry period, the villagers saw some black bucks, which the villagers had never seen before. Immediately thereafter, there was heavy downpour breaking the dry spell. There was bumper crop and this famine ended.

This led people to believe that misfortune may fall on the villages, if these animals do not stay in their villages. Hence, they do not kill them and even some of the animals come to the villagers, as they were confident that local people won't do anything. But they take to flight when they saw a stranger in pant and shirt distinctly different from bare bodied villagers with *dhoti*.

They were so attached to this animal that as the story goes in early part of the century; the villagers caught a British Collector for poaching one black buck and punished him by extracting a fine and asking him to bury the carcass. A similar incident did take place during my tenure, when relations of a local police officer did poaching. They could not provide any resistance, afraid of reprisal. But they reported the fact to the local Range Officer, who seized the skin and prosecuted those involved.

Of course lot of trouble had to be faced by our staff, till intervention of the Govt. and Senior Police Officers. That is a long story.

But the younger generations are less and less attached to the species and the animals seldom stray towards Babanpur near Aska, where the people do not have any attachment towards them, nor do they have any such faith.

We conducted a census of the species in 1980 in the main concentration. It was a direct count, as it was a flat open ground. We devised our own technique of census. Each enumerator carried 3 little bamboo baskets on their waist and a pouch of gravels. They counted all animals' sex wise and by putting pebbles in the respective basket meant for male, female or young ones whose sex could not be determined. Each enumerator, made to walk 1 furlong apart, perpendicular to the road, counted animals on his right strip only. The animals running to another strip was not counted. We counted 485 of them.

Such a large number of animals moving in the agricultural fields could destroy their entire crop. Of course, they cause considerable loss when crops are young. But, as these animals are 'fine feeders', they depended on the very young succulent seedlings of different crops or fine grasses in meadows and field bunds. As the crop started growing, and became coarse, they never attempted to browse them. They never went to the forest, as they neither needed any overhead shed nor could take any coarse vegetation of the forest. Though the Forest department provided some support in the form of meadow development, waterhole etc, their security continues to be mainly the responsibility of the local community. Besides, Bhetanoi and Buguda area, there were smaller herds near Kabisuryanagar in Ganjam around Jauguda, Krishnagiri forest, coastal sandy stretches near Chilika and Konark- Balukhand sanctuary near Konark.

If the people take responsibility in protecting any animal, their future can be quite safe, even without any Government protection. Thanks to such efforts, their number has multiplied in the state and their range has spread to new areas. But sadly the population in Balukhand has been wiped out. Efforts are on to reintroduce them there. This is another case similar to the conservations efforts of Vishnoi community of Rajasthan, who respect 29 principles of non-violence. Many more communities should come forward to protect the rich biodiversity of this country, which is said to be one of twelve mega diversity region of the world, despite its high population and cattle density.

15

BHOLA THE MAKHNA

It is a tradition among rich people in northern part of the Bihar and Eastern Uttar Pradesh to rear elephants and lend them to *Mahauts* on payment of a monthly rent. The Mahauts take these elephants and go in small groups to places of pilgrimage in different parts of the country. They go round the villages from house to house and to small shops. The people, particularly Hindus, who respect elephants as elephant headed God Ganesh, the god of learning and *Vahana* (carrier) of Laxmi, the goddess of wealth feed them with coconuts, bananas, paddy, sweets etc. and give money, when they bless them or their children with their trunks. The earnings from this meets the cost of upkeep of the animals, food for the *mahaut*, and monthly payment of rent to the owner, besides surplus earning for the mahaut to be sent to their families back home and saving for the lean months. Many such animals visit Odisha as the temple of Lord Jagannath is situated here in Puri on the eastern coast of the Bay of Bengal. This is considered as one of the 4 *dhams* meaning exulted places of Hindu pilgrimage. In north and western India the elephants usually form part of marriage procession of the rich and sometimes religious processions.

Bhola was one such elephant who was coming from Varanasi and unlike most of such wandering elephants majority of whom were females, this one was male but without any tusk. He was a 'makhna' meaning a male without tusk. Among Asian elephants only males have tusks, but makhnas are tusk less. But in very rare cases the females possess small tusks which are called *'tushes'*. These females are called *'Sankhini'* in Sanskrit. Males are usually avoided by these wandering groups, as they are large and powerful, often ill tempered, need more food and sometimes go completely out of control, when they pass through a phase of sexual excitation called *'musth'*. During this period lasting for 2 to 3 weeks, particularly in winter they do not obey commands, exude a fluid from their temples and often charge their own keepers. Many instances of their killing mahauts have been reported from all over the country and other Asian countries.

Bhola was on his way with his keeper to Puri through Sambalpur. It was perhapsMarch, 1986. This *'makhna'* was an unusually large and well built animal. When, he was approaching Sambalpur City from Hirakud, he charged his *mahaut*, who fled away leaving him alone with no one to control. He trampled over an old beggar, killing him on the spot and went on rampage, in and around Sambalpur. Vigil by the police force did not improve the situation. He went inside Ainthapalli police station campus following the police force and upturned a jeep and damaged few other vehicles parked there. People were panic stricken. The wildlife warden Sri S. C. Bohidar sent frantic messages to the Chief Wildlife Warden for help. We had tranquilizing drugs and equipments. Sri B. N. Nayak and Sri Hansda, then A.C.F.s of Similipal Tiger Project were immediately directed to proceed. Bhola, the Makhna kept on wandering in low denuded hills on the outskirts of the city. Sri Nayak succeeded in darting this animal and tied him up with a thick sisal rope to a *Mohwa* tree on Rourkela road about 5 km from the Sambalpur city.

But the ordeal did not end there. It was yet to begin. As he was pretty close to the road he kept on standing on the busy highway and charged passing vehicles. The District Administration was puzzled not knowing how to handle this extraordinary situation. I talked to the Collector Sri Mohan Kumar over phone and assured him that I am immediately leaving for Sambalpur and shall be doing our best to take 'Bhola' to a place away from the road.

I proceeded to Sambalpur. Before that the district administration did its best to locate its owner and *mahaut*, but could not get any trace of them. They did not want to be identified for the fear that, they may have to face legal problem, as their elephant had caused excessive damage, killed a person and caused panic. Hence the Collector was its lawful custodian under the Cattle Trespass Act as a domestic elephant was then treated as 'cattle' as per law in force.

Immediately on my arrival at Sambalpur I proceeded straight to see Bhola, chained and tied to a lone tree very close to the Highway. Lot of people had gathered around the animal, which appeared to be in the waning stage of 'musth'. Though part of the road was free, the drivers were very scared as he could reach a vehicle though his trunk, when he stretched himself. He was fed with *Ficus* branches and supplied water for drinking and water was thrown on him to keep him cool. I went round the area to locate a proper water body to shift him away from the road. I was happy to see a tank with good depth about two hundred meters away from the road with number of old large shady trees strong enough for trying Bhola and for providing necessary shade.

But I knew that the task ahead was easier said than done. Shifting a huge erratic 4- ton animal with massive strength, without any keeper needed proper planning, manpower, discipline and guts. But it has to be done fast. I got into a discussion with the wildlife warden who was also the D.F.O., Sri Nayak, Sri Hansda and other forest officers and prepared a list of requirements for the operation. I decided to start the operation at 4.00 in the next morning. I requested the district administration and police for sixty policemen in their morning drill attire, a pair of elephants from a circus then playing at Jharsuguda, about 300 meters of sisal rope from the State Electricity Board and some policemen to keep the crowd disciplined. I visited the site again made up my mind about the operation. But I could hardly sleep that night. A tent was also sent for pitching at the site for taking rest during the operation.

It was pitch dark at that hour of dawn around 4.00 A.M., when we reached the site and saw the elephant's, huge frame in the headlight of the jeep looking like a huge brownish boulder. As we went closer, he appeared to be calmer and exhausted. He loudly exhaled air through his trunk and made a loud "phang......phang......" sound while hitting the tree trunk making a sound like beating of a bundle of paddy straw on a empty metallic tube. He was obviously enraged, though tired.

Though we were first to arrive, all our men and materials kept on reaching the site at regular intervals including the two elephants from the circus party. A briefing session was to follow; as any mistake on anyone's part could be fatal. We decided to sedate the animal with 'xylazene' before we started tying him up with the long sisal rope and tie to a tree 200 meters away and then pull the animal with 60 police men while prodding him from behind with two elephants and our mahauts. The ground was flat and slushy. He was injected sedative at around 5.00 a.m. and the rope was tied up and the operation started. He refused to budge an inch. A tractor was also engaged to pull him. It dragged him by about 5 meters like a dragging a wooden horse. When he stopped and did not budge and let out a trumpeting sound the circus elephants were very scared and tried to flee. Ahead was a high tension line. We could sense that if he can reach the line the entire area, which was slushy, would have been charged through his body resulting in a very serious accident. We had to stop the operation and sent out request for disconnecting the line. It did take some time, but it was done. When we commenced our operation again the sedation was waning off slowly. We prodded him to step ahead with the two elephants on either side. But the powerful 'makhna' drove the two elephants by pushing them aside, which were about half a meter shorter than him in height. So strong were the pushes on either side that they ran with their *mahauts* on their back and refused to come close to Bhola. We had by then crossed about 100 meters.

He again stood firm with his forelegs stretched to the front and refused to budge. It was already afternoon, people were very hungry. We had some tea and snacks. We decided to pull and push all at a time. The jeep was put on fore-wheel drive gear and put behind the elephant and the entire force was put in to operation. This did work; the elephant moved forward in short bursts of few meters at a time. We avoided using excessive force to avoid injury to him. He finally reached the tank bund at 4.00 pm, almost 12 hours after the operation started. It was a safe place where he had good shade, water and the motorists were safe on the highway. The local forest officials looked after him with mahauts from Nandankanan for about a month or so. People of Sambalpur heaved a sigh of relief.

Bhola continued to be kept at Sambalpur for more than a month, when the local staff found it difficult to manage him and requested for shifting him to Nandankanan as he was quite often erratic.

I was in favour of keeping him away from Nandankanan, as this park was visited by about 4000 visitors every day. Besides, large number of animals and staff were staying in the park. If he is unmanageable there, it may be difficult for managing him without serious accidents. But, against my views it was brought to Nandankanan on the 15th, June, 1986, despite a tragic attack on people on his way from Sambalpur. I decided to keep him under a large banyan tree near the western gate away from the rest of our other captive elephants, as he could harm them during *'musth'*, which was rather unusually frequent with him. Besides proximity to cow elephants always activated him to go in to 'musth'; which was other reason to keep him away from the crowded area. Of course, we decided to bring other cow elephants closer to him at intervals for company, as that could help influence his behaviour. But he appeared to be perpetually in a state of excitement. He also exhibited peculiar behaviour of probing the anal cavity of the cow elephants with his trunk and taking out excreta for eating. He also indulged in throwing branches at people going close to him and also tried to snap the two ropes tied to his hind leg by urinating on them and pulling hard.

He was remaining relatively quiet for four days or so and was again coming to 'musth'. The flow of musth fluid was very high. Such unusual phenomenon was not found mention in any literature I had assessed on elephant. We spent many sleepless nights watching him in pitch darkness with pouring rain. Staff kept a whole night vigil. About 2 months passed before he broke his chain from both the hind legs and started running all around in the 5 sq.km. park. Even he crossed the Kanjia take, a shallow lake separating the zoo from the botanical garden and went to Botanical Garden. Our staff followed him on elephant back and others followed on foot. His movement was erratic. We were afraid that he could break the enclosure of any large cat, most of whom lived in the park in open air enclosures and lion safari. The rhinos, other elephants and bears were other causes of concern. Secondly the visitors and staff could get trampled. The people were afraid of coming to the park while staff decided to avoid going close to Bhola. Teams were formed to follow with tranquilizing equipments and guns. But he was so restless, fast and erratic that it was not possible to get a clear close view. Teams were stationed at vantage points all around the park to report his movement. Even food was sent to each team as they had continued to toil for more than 18 hours. They were all very very tired.

'Bhola' trying to break the Safari gate.

We had to be prepared to face any eventuality and requested Dr. G. P. Mohanty an ace hunter to come prepared with his 500 express rifle. Bhola did not sober down and charged the main gate of the lion safari and bent the same. Everyone was scared that any further attack with force on safari will be dangerous, as the lions could come out in to the open. He was scared away from there in to the 'nature trial', a forty hectare patch to natural forest enclosed with 2 ½ mt. high chain link fence meant for herbivores. After prolonged discussion it was felt that there is no alternative left other than to eliminate the 'makhna'. The Chief Wildlife Warden Sri R. N. Mohanty declared Bhola 'dangerous to human life' under Section 11 of Wildlife (Protection) Act 1971 and requested Dr. Mohanty, who was a surgeon by profession and had long experience of handling dangerous animals, to hunt down. It was a painful decision taken after weighting all options. Despite reluctance of all in the park this painful decision was to be taken to save human and other animal lives. To make situation worse, it was a 'Thursday' the day of Goddess Laxmi, whose carrier was elephant.

Dr. Mohanty also found it dangerous to stalk the charging 'makhna' on foot and sat on a docile cow elephant and proceeded in to the 'nature trial' with his rifle loaded. He met 'Bhola' in a small opening in the forest at around 12.30 in the afternoon and planted the shot on his temple. He dropped on the ground with one single shot. This tragic end came on the 13th, September, 1986. Though everyone was very sad, there was relief among the families of staff, local villagers and visitors. End of makhna came about a kilometer away from his adopted home.

This huge elephant might have been bought from Sonepur cattle fair *(mela)* of Bihar. This is the largest fair in the country and perhaps in Asia, located in the confluence of Rivers Ganga and Gandak where different cattle and other animals including domestic elephants are sold in the month of November-December. Buyers come from different parts of the country, particularly northern part of India. This fair is also known as Harihar *mela* and is reported to be dating back to 3rd centuryBC. It is said that even buyers from far off countries of central Asia were reported to be coming here in the past to buy elephants. Of course in recent years, due to rigid enforcement of Wildlife (Protection) Act, 1972 the flow of elephants to the fair has come down drastically to ensure that wild elephants are not captured for domestication. Only captive born elephants with proper documentation were sold here till recently.

Perhaps Bhola could have been saved and roamed freely in the forest helping to the improve status of the elephants in the wild. The elephant population is threatened in India, as tuskers are being poached for their tusks which fetch very high price in clandestine international market. In southern states of Tamilnadu, Kerala and Karnataka, the ratio between tuskers and cows is diminishing very fast at alarming rate. Of course '*makhnas*' in the wild are relatively safe. This slaughter has started in last decade or so in some eastern states. Females are also not safe as their habitat in shrinking and they are also subjected to electrocution, injury by crop protection guns or bows and arrows and poisoning; a result of human elephant conflict. Let us leave them alone in their habitat and preserve their habitat so that this magnificent animal can continue to move in this subcontinent for centuries to come. While domestic elephants can continue to be used in different activities like forest protection, eco-tourism, forestry and other works in a humane way, it is certainly undignified for the largest land mammal to be used for begging as was done with Bhola and being done with many more of them. I am not against capture of excess population from any habitat which is over populated beyond sustenance, as a part of scientific wildlife management. But the captive population also has to be managed well with least possible cruelty as per a proper elephant management practice during its active age, as is done by Kerala, Tamilnadu and other state Forest Departments. They can be given well deserved pension and rest in their old age.

16

A SAD END

Entire tract of Sukinda area of newly formed Jajpur district and adjoining Daitari area of Keonjhar district, part of hill range of Eastern ghats is sitting on some of richest mineral deposits of the country. There are chromite deposits and iron ore which are mined for the local plants and export through Paradeep Port. An express highway now converted to National Highway had been constructed more than four decades back exclusively to carry the ore to this port town for onward shipping to Japan. The red soil of the region also supported a rich deciduous forest with predominantly Sal trees. More than four decades of mining, road development, colonies for labor force, mineral dumps, ore handing plants, railway lines and ropeways have all played their role in honey combing the contiguous deep forest of the area. But despite that many patches still hold good forest mainly due to their difficult terrain, making it inaccessible to the timber smugglers. Some natural or planted vegetation has also come up on the dumps of over burden soil, which has been removed from the top of the deposits for mining them. Though many parts in the area where township or laborer settlements have come up are buzzing with activity, there are many relatively quiet green hilly patches, which behold unparallel scenic beauty.

I received a phone call from the Range officer, Anandapur that he has heard of a tiger or leopard getting trapped somewhere near Daitari and lot of people have gathered in the area. He could not give me the detail as that was not a part of his range. I thought that, it can possibly be a leopard and gave advice to our staff to immediately proceed for rescuing it.

But in the evening it was confirmed that it was a full grown Royal Bengal Tiger, which has got caught in a snare on a precipitous slope created by iron ore mining, far away from any habitation. I was told that it is impossible to rescue this animal unless he is tranquilized by experts and crated. I had no time to spare. It was almost midnight. I neither had a transport nor was Nandankanan zoo telephone working. I contacted the D.F.O. of Nandankanan, Sri Abhimanyu Behera designated as Wildlife Conservation Officer. He appreciated the urgency and immediately took his scooter and managed to reach Nandankanan. A team was immediately formed of a Veterinarian, tranquilizing team headed by Sri Purohit, Forest Ranger, keepers of tiger exhibits and other support staff.

They also located a sturdy steel crate in the store for crating the animal. They started much before dawn, as I told them that every single minute is crucial, as the tiger is struggling for life and perhaps the wire rope is eating into his flesh with every jerk he exerts to escape. He is without food and water, no one knows for how many hours and must have been badly dehydrated.

As this team reached there at about 6.30a.m., a crowd had already gathered there along with the local forest staff and onlookers. The tiger was growling and trying hard to escape from the snare. But he was injuring himself more and more. It was in a difficult terrain. The snare was made of discarded wire rope, usually used in mining practice, set along animal track used regularly by the wild boars which were proliferating in this area that was abandoned after mining. Because of producing large litters, their number in the area had gone up. They dig up earth to make it easy for them to look for roots and tubers taken by them as food. Perhaps this tiger followed a herd of wild boars, which is also one of its preferred preys and got entangled in the snare. The wild boars might have escaped, as they would have ran helter skelter seeing the tiger following them.

No one dared to go close to the tiger as three of his legs were free and he was a huge animal. Finding no other way to transfer him to a cage, Purohit darted him with 'xylazene' which numbed him at first and then completely sedated him. Then he was transferred to the steel cage taken from Nandankanan. He was administered antibiotics through intramuscular injection and quickly shifted to Nandankanan. His leg was swollen to 4 times its normal size. He was groaning with pain. Immediately on his arrival at Nandankanan I saw him and advised to treat his injuries etc. and transfer to the intensive care unit of the veterinary hospital.

Nest morning at about 9.00 a.m. he was transferred to a squeeze cage, where we saw him limping. This device was used for facilitating close examination and treatment. Such squeeze cages were standard equipments for zoos and very useful in handling large cats without chemical immobilization. This has adjustable side walls, which presses the animal between the two walls so that it cannot move its limbs and the veterinarian can handle an animal with ease.

But, to the surprise and shock of everybody, he succumbed to his injuries. He was declared dead.

As in case of all zoo animals wild animal carcasses are subjected to post mortem examination. Such examination gives a lot of information to the zoo management for upkeep and treatment of animals, including infectious diseases, if any or other causes of death. His body was also subjected to the same process.

In this case the area around the shoulder was full of blood clots including a portion on his hind quarters. The prolonged period of pulling without food and water caused internal hemorrhage, dehydration etc. which became fatal. Yet another majestic animal met his sad end, despite all attempts to save him.

It was told that there was also a female in the area with her two cubs. It is not known if this was the last male in the area and with this patchy and highly disturbed forest it would have been difficult to get a mate. The fragmented forest areas have caused this problem. As far as Orissa is concerned, except for tigers in Similipal, Satkosia gorge and Sunabeda, other tigers are more or less isolated. The forests are getting more and more fragmented and exposed to anthropogenic pressures. Though the Project Tiger started in 1973 had been able take the tiger number 3700 to 4000, they had drastically reduced in number a decade or so back. Of course recent status surveys are relatively more encouraging. They are mostly found in the tiger reserves. In other fragmented areas they are losing ground very fast. In my opinion, unless action is taken to save and improve the tiger habitats in and outside the tiger reserves immediately they may permanently lose their struggle for survival as India is the largest remaining tiger habitat in the world now.

17

PYTHON AND CHEETALS

Bhitarkanika National Park, located in the estuary of Brahmani and Baitarani Rivers of Odisha, is a mud flat that supports India's richest mangrove biodiversity. These tidal swamps, inundated twice a day, also have very rich faunal diversity in the form of mammals, reptiles, birds, amphibians and insects. Though a very small patch nestled in the northern most corner of newly formed Kendrapara district and criss-crossed by meandering rivers, rivulets and creeks, it can be called a nature's paradise. About 20 years of protection efforts since 1975, when it was first given the status of a sanctuary mainly for conservation of estuarine crocodile known locally as *'Baula'*. Despite heavy demographic pressures from local residents, also the absentee land-lords living elsewhere and migrants from neighboring state of West Bengal and even Bangladesh, some pockets have survived the onslaught and have supported myriads of life-forms. Some of them are fishing cats, cheetals, sambars, dolphins, estuarine crocodiles, water monitor lizards, yellow monitor lizards, pythons, king cobras, vultures, kites, variety of king- fishers, white ibis, open billed storks, painted storks, grey herons, purple herons, egrets, terns, bar headed geese, other migratory birds, many species of crabs including the blue-blooded horse shoe crabs, hermit crabs, mudskippers and other mollusks and many species of fishes. Sixty-three species of mangrove vegetation thriving here is the highest among any mangrove habitats of the country. Bhitarkanika forest block and adjoining Dangmal area are said to be the core of this small but beautiful National Park. The main Forest Rest House and other tourism facilities besides the Crocodile Research and Conservation Unit and the administrative office of Kanika range are located here. Though there is peak visitor actively here in winter months, the early autumn months are usually not very crowded. There is a grassy opening all around these facilities for the benefit of the herbivores, particularly cheetal, who visit this meadow every evening and graze in spite of all human activity. Of course, the sense of security provided by the entire complex besides the succulent grass encourages them to visit this grass land. They feel more secure as they can see the predators like crocodile and pythons from a distance to avoid going close to them. With the day break they go back to the surrounding forests. This patch of meadow also gets inundated by tidal waters during high tide. After the tide reduces the water flows down to the rivers giving a magical effect of several hill streams cascading down. It is a wonderful feeling.

The Cheetals attacking the Python.

119

It was a dawn like any autumn day, where the staff staying in Dangmal complex, heard a very unusual commotion of alarm calls from Cheetals, many at a time 'ah' 'ah' 'ah' which reverberated in the otherwise tranquil environment. Some birds nearby also responded. A lone hanuman languor, one of very few in the park also responded *"hooon, hoon"* and *"khe…..khe"* *"khe…khe…..khe"*. The staff could not know what has happened. Many rushed to the site and found a large herd of about 70 cheetals standing in very close formation and looking at a particular direction. The Forest Guard and Dhumal, a very daring forest helper could not believe what they saw. Dhumal was like a wild animal himself when it comes to his encounters with wild animals. Once during an encounter with a king cobra, tip of his nose was hit by a king cobra. His poison was deadly as this is the most venomous of all the Indian snakes. As he knew that it will be fatal, he lost no time to chop off tip of his nose and bunt the wound with lighted *bidi* (country cigarette wrapped with a leaf). This daring act saved his life. They found few individuals of the herd stamping on a huge Python that had swallowed some animal. The stags attacked with their antlers down. How could have this happened? What was the provocation? They went closer to have a very close look and saw the snake vomiting something large and slimy.

It was a cheetal fawn, which was still alive and was moving its limbs. They brought both the python and the fawn to the center and tried to treat them. But the stamping by so many cheetals together had punctured holes in the python's head and body, battering it. He died within an hour. The asphyxia was also too much for the little fawn who could not be saved.

Quite often the human kind talks and tries to prove that he is very intelligent and can unite to face a calamity. This incident enacted deep inside the forest away from human civilization opened my eyes, when I heard of the incident. They certainly knew that this python has taken one of their young ones and they need punish him and rescue the young one. They also perhaps knew that, though python is their main predator on the ground in this ecosystem, it cannot attack them when they are in a herd and more so when he is immobile due to swallowing of the young cheetal. It was difficult to explain, but true. Many a dramas like this are enacted by different animals in the wilderness far away from human notice every day. Unless we protect these little patches of wild habitat may be forests, wetlands, deserts or high hills, such plays shall stop being enacted making human life even poorer. Their contributions of intangible benefits for supporting different life forms on the earth are enormous.

--------------- ✦✦✦✦✦ ---------------

18

AGASTHI, THE
ADORABLE TUSKER

It was a winter night and we were chasing a tusker barely visible in the dim moon light and fading torch lights, through harvested paddy fields, falling, crossing high field bunds, bruising ourselves and tearing our dresses to the accompaniment uncharitable words used by junior staff, also in tow at a distance. This was last effort by us led by Sri S.R.Choudhury to recapture a problem wild tusker.

I came to Ganjam in 1974 February from Kalahandi where I was looking after the working of Kendu leaf (Tendu patta in Hindi) used extensively in South Asian countries as wrapper for handmade cheap cigarettes. First four years of my stay in southern district of Ganjam, which was earlier a part of Madras presidency, later merged with the new State of Orissa, now Odisha, carved out of Bihar and Orissa, Madras and Central Province (now M.P.) in 1936, was spent for taking up plantation work as DFO, Afforestation. This was followed by six months of commercial planting of cashew nuts for the Orissa Forest Corporation which was found in

1962as the first such corporation in the country. I shifted to Bhanjanagar from Berhampur in 1978 and look change of Ghumsur South Division earlier known as Berhampur Division. Most of the eastern part of this Division close to Bay of Bengal was rather devoid of any forest growth and was a rich agricultural tract. People there are very hard working and many of them go to far off places like Assam, Gujarat and Punjab for working in tea gardens, textile mills, diamond cutting outfits, construction projects or agricultural work. Only the Western and North Eastern corners of the division had some good forests and fewer people. Elephants were known to inhabit Western parts of the division around Surada.

Odisha, earlier known as Kalinga was historically famous for its war elephants had a small population of about 2000 elephants out of about 25,000 in the country left, most of whom inhabited the three southern states and north-east. Out of these 2000 odd elephants most lived on the north of river Mahanadi, which dissects Odisha in to two distinct parts. Highest concentration of elephants was in Similipal and its surrounding, with almost one fourth of the total population living there. Among the southern part, Kalahandi, Chandrapur and Lakhari Valley tract had maximum population and many areas did not have any elephant population left.

Similarly the plain agricultural and thickly populated tract of Berhampur, Chatrapur, Aska, dotted with small highly degraded low hills with bush like bamboo clumps, had no elephant habitat left. A small hill range of Kerandimal between Berhampur, Digapahandi and Chikiti triangle had some scrub forest left with very exposed rocky surface with small patches of cashew nut plantations. This situation had further aggravated due to intensive grazing of cattle, particularly very large herds of goats. But, it was reported by local people and forest staff that two bull elephants lived here mainly depending on scrubby bamboo forest and agricultural crops raised by local people. One of them was a large bull with large tusks, very cool in temperament while the other, a small bull with very small tusks was rather short tempered and often chased the people, particularly those who go to the forest for grazing their cows and goats or for collecting fuel wood and bamboo. Such unattached male duos were reported by several wild-lifers. I never thought that they can stay in such scanty forest which has no link left with any other elephant habitat. The nearest one was Lakhari Valley some 50 Kilometers away. The scanty forest and crop raised by locals in the boulder strewn poor soil of Kerandimal was perhaps not sufficient to sustain these two pachyderms. While the smaller and timid one did not venture out of these forests, the larger one did go out of the forest in to the agriculture rich tracts of Ganjam plains for scouting and raiding crops of paddy, maize, sugar cane, groundnut, betel and even potatoes while hiding in isolated mango, cashew and bamboo grooves during the day.

It was one such raiding spree during which this tusker covered more than fifty kilometers out of his forest abode and even crossed the two of the towns of the district, Berhampur, the main city and the district headquarters and reached the banks of Rushikulya River. He started raiding crops, broke hedges, destroyed homestead gardens and when chased by villagers, particularly the younger ones with fire, crackers, drums and even boulders he used to mock-charge and in the process sometimes damaged houses. There was strong demand from the people to shoot him down, as no other means was available to them. One winter night on the 20th December, 1981 the Collector of the district Sri G.B. Mukherjee gave me a ring and informed me that the animal has become difficult to handle and needed to be shot down. For this he needed permission from the Forest Department to hunt him down through the police. The Wildlife (Protection) Act 1972 had already come in to force in the State since 1974 and under this it was essential that any animal in the Schedule-I of the Act has to be declared dangerous to human life or properly by the Chief Wildlife Warden of the State. All animals which were considered endangered in their status were placed in Schedule-I.

I as Wildlife Warden of the district was quite alarmed and requested him to wait till I reach and see the animal. But, I wanted him to organize a police contingent to help me to handle the animal and keep the people at a distance from him.

Next morning I located the animal near Chatrapur being harassed by people stoning from all sides. It was even difficult for him to find a way to escape. In the process he was entering villages, backyard gardens, breaking fences, cow-sheds etc. People were shouting, gesticulating, throwing gravels using catapults and even hurling burning wooden pieces. He was trumpeting and giving mock -charges of 20-30 meters to scare away people and then stepping back. He was getting some respite for some time as he left one village limit to go to the next to be replaced by next group of villagers. But he was not harming anybody; through they went very close to the animal. All effort by our forest staff failed to restrain the people. Their number sometimes swelled to more than a thousand.

I thought it proper to requisition a strong police contingent to keep the people at bay and make a horse shoe pattern with organized police and forest personnel and give him a direction to go back to the forest from where he came. The district police administration agreed to our suggestions and sent a contingent consisting of 33 police personnel. This police team was led by a young and enthusiastic Addl. Superintendent of Police named Sri Anup Patnaik, who before joining the Indian Police Service also had a stint in Indian Forest Service, while I led the whole team including forest personnel. We could successfully keep the people away from the tusker when we formed a horse shoe pattern formation around the elephant with an opening towards south-east, the direction of the distant forest from where he came. The movement for first few kilometers through the cultivated field, now without any crop, village roads, small dry streams, orchards, Casurina plantations was quite slow, as he used to pause, turn back, stop and take dust bath. But when he could get the message clear that we shall not slop till he returns to his forest habitat. He moved faster towards his forest home and left us far behind. On 23rd, December, '81 we watched him vanish in the distant horizon, out of our view. We were relieved that he is saved from death sentence.

Few months passed, during which we did not hear anything about him. Perhaps, he continued with his younger friend in Kerandimal forest. It was on the 30th, January'1982 I heard of him again from Bada Kusasthali of Chhatrapur area. In the meantime I had contacted Sri S. R. Choudhury, Field Director, Similipal Tiger Reserve to ascertain if tranquillizing equipments and drugs are with him and if it is possible to tranquilize and capture this tusker if he does not stop raiding crops. One of the most practical field wildlife experts in the country then, he was known never to back out from any challenge faced by him. He had a few chemical immobilizations of injured elephants to his credit earlier, besides tranquilizing large cats while teaching wildlife management to the trainees in Dehradun. He was very sad as he had just lost his pet tigress Khairi, who lived with him for seven years in the Forest Rest House at Jasipur and went with him wherever he went. Though he was advancing in age and had still not recovered from the shock of death of Khairi, whom he had to shoot as she had rabies; he accepted the challenge and told me to inform him when he comes out again. I had already organized a team of forest staff of my division, who trailed the animal round the clock observing his movement and activity. He kept on moving around Chatrapur up to Rushikulya river right up to the coastal casuarinas, cashew nut and Polanga (*Calophylum*) plantations raised by the government as a part of coastal shelter belt to minimize effect of coastal cyclone and those raised by people for putting their sandy stretches of land to economic production. He was taking rest in the mango, casuarinas, cashew and bamboo grooves to escape harassment by the people of the villages. His daily movements were recorded and reported to the Divisional Office. I informed Mr. Choudhury over telephone that, the huge tusker is being trailed and now is the time when one can tranquilize the animal. The animal was moving on either side of the National Highway in the cashew plantation and mango grooves north of Chatrapur. I was personally following the movement of this animal on foot with my staff. We had no *'kumki'* (elephant specially trained for elephant capture and training) elephant nor there was any capture of elephant after our independence in the state. He knew that he is being trailed. So stealthy was his movement that many a times, he was just about 1 meter behind me. I could not feel his presence. But he never harmed us. These hide and seek continued for several hours even on 10th, February, before Sri Choudhury reached at around 2.30PM. He was in jungle green, his usual field attire, accompanied by Miss Nihar Swain, his fair cousin with his tranquilizing equipment of dist-inject gun and pistol and imported narcotic drug called M.99 (Etrophine hydrochloride). I was told that one has to take adequate precaution while using this narcotic drug as if a drop of it goes in to the blood stream of a man it can be fatal as its potency was known to be 10,000 times higher than Morphine. Hence before the drug is loaded into a syringe, its antidote named M.50.50 was loaded and sufficient supply of water was kept handy to wash off the drug if required. Gloves are used for loading. However there was no time to lose as evening was approaching when this animal was spotted near Agasthi Nuagaon, a coastal village. The wind was blowing from south to north and hence we decided to position ourselves on the north of the trail, which the animal was likely to follow if prodded. The gun and pistol were cleaned a loaded. It is like a two stage rocket launcher where a metal tube is loaded with the drug and fitted with a needle and a feather stabilizer behind. Between the stabilizer and the drug there was a small charge. A cartridge is also loaded in the pistol behind the projectile assembly called 'canule'. The cartridge explodes when trigger is pressed pushing the canule to its destination. When it hits the subject its impact causes the second explosion in the 'canule' and the drug is pushed in to the body of the animal.

As per plan the elephant followed the predicted track. Sri Choudhury, ready with his loaded gun pressed the trigger when he found that the distance was right at about 4.00PM. A very accomplished marksman, his shot was perfect and hit the tusker on his rump. He ran at a breakneck speed though the village, due east in to the coastal casuarinas plantation trailed by village children. We also followed. Village boys who were following the pachyderm sprinted back and informed us that the animal has fallen down inside the casuarinas and cashew plantation almost after an hour of being darted. We ran with the people and the forest staff in that direction as none of us had earlier seen such an operation. We were ready for the operation with chains, u-bolts and sisal ropes. As he was still not fully sedated to be safely handled, he was injected further dose of M-99 and Acepromazine before tying him up. We had to work fast as Sri Choudhury told us that we should revive the animal within 2 hours. His body temperature, pulse etc. were being monitored. His two hind legs were chained and in turn tied to a number of casuarina trees, as we knew the strength of the elephant, which could easily uproot a casuarina tree from its sandy base. Some banana, coconut and ficus branches were procured to feed him after his recovery and several buckets of water were also brought. By that time night had descended on us. We arranged for camping of staff. After the preliminaries, all were asked to clear the area and M 50-50; the antidote to M-99 was injected in to the veins in his ear lobe. At first there was movement of his ears, then the tail and trunk and in about forty minutes he stood up still drowsy with hundreds of people watching him. A naming ceremony followed, out of several names suggested 'Agasthi' found acceptance as he was captured from Agasthi-Nuagan'. He slowly accepted water and food and was very calm. We were very jubilant through tired. Sri Choudhury who was about 57 had already performed a long jeep Journey from Jashipur before running behind the elephant. After setting up the camp with adequate food, lighting etc. we both left for Berhampur by around 1.00AM to return next morning.

Though we were triumphant about the achievement, many thoughts crossed my mind. What to do next? Where to keep him? How to train? But we went to bed early to start the next day very early and reach Agasthi by dawn and show him to the district officials who pressed for his elimination.

We got up at four in the morning. Finished our morning work in a jiffy and proceeded to see Agasthi. As we approached the village people, who were waiting for us informed that Agasthi has escaped. He had broken the chain and fled. We saw his foot prints for some distance. Thereafter there was no trace or any news from anywhere. We arranged jeeps and fanned out in all directions, looking for foot prints and information from villagers. But there was none. We consulted the topographical maps of the area, looking for any thicket where he might be hiding. Could he trace his way back to the forest? It was ruled out, as he could not cover that distance without being noticed. Lastly we saw a large bamboo brake of about 50 hectors, surrounded by dry open fields without any crop as they had been harvested. Inside was completely dark and there was no human activity there. This can be a perfect hiding place. Sri Choudhury suggested that we go there. We perambulated around the grove to look for any foot print. There were none except some very old ones imprinted when the soil was wet. Sri Choudhury lost all hopes of getting him there. At that time, as I was looking through one of dark tunnels formed by the bamboo clumps two glistening write tusks appeared about 20 meters away from us. I told the Field Director what I saw. But surprisingly, when he looked they were not there. He obviously could sense about our presence and was trying to avoid eye contact. I insisted that we load the gun and pistol immediately as it was getting dark. We cautiously went in to the grove and saw his huge dark form through an opening. The first dart hit him on upper part of his rump near the back. He brushed against a clump and removed the canule and marched ahead. As he was walking out a second shot from the pistol hit his jump as he walked out of the brake in to the to the open fields brightly lit by the late afternoon sun. As he was negotiating a high field bund, he fell down in a sitting position with his chest on the ground and lost consciousness. Sri Choudhury's immediate worry was the position where 'Agasthi' was lying. As elephant's heart is on the lower side of his chest his massive 3 ½ tons of weight could stop his heart function unless the position is changed. This needed a lot of manpower to roll him to a side. This has to be done fast. We had very few staff that had converged on the site from different directions. But this was far away from any village and darkness was fast descending. Rolling him to a side also had its own problem as his massive head was hanging down from a field bund, where his neck was resting.

Hence there was need for people, some brush wood or other padding to support his massive head and some good lighting arrangement for the operation of tying him, revival and arrangement of food. There was also necessity of setting up a camp at the site for round the clock vigil.

We sent out people to call the villagers, with some axes, firewood bundles for support, lanterns and brighter *Petromax* kerosene lights. We had number of torches with us.

Number of people gathered in about half an hour. We had to act very fast. We requested people help us to roll the tusker lying like a massive rock. None of them dared to touch him due to the fear that Agasthi might attack them. I had to go and sit on his limp body to give them the confidence that he will not attack. Slowly all of them young and old started pushing him and rolled him to his right side. Before that few bundles of firewood was placed below the place where his head was to rest comfortably. Having achieved this, the next step was to secure him to a strong post or tree with sisal ropes. There was no tree nearby. But there were several massive bamboo clumps. This appeared to be quite strong to hold the animal. We decided to use few adjacent clumps, as we had sufficient length of sisal ropes for the purpose. His hind legs were chained and it was tied to few bamboo clumps taking the rope round the clumps. Time was precious. It was necessary to revive him fast. All people were asked to clear the area and all objects were shifted before M 50-50 the drug to neutralize M-99 was injected intravenously by Sri Choudhury in his ear lobe. He got up in 5 minutes after moving the tail, rolling the eyes and flapping the ears. He stood still for some time. Then drank water from the bucket, took some bananas and oranges. We took the lights away from him and slept on cots made of ropes. After an hour or so, he started pulling the rope, to set free. He pulled hard, resting his body on two fore legs and trunk and applied all the force allowing his hind legs to stretch hanging from the rope, so that the weight of his entire body also stretches the rope. He made repeated attempts, but to no avail, as the sisal rope was very strong. He also tried to moisten the rope with water and urine before trying hard to snap the rope. The ropes and chain held. We maintained vigil during the entire night. He was much quieter as the morning sun flooded the fields with golden sunshine. His feeding, watering, spraying water started in full swing. It was in the evening, I planned to stay for the night giving much needed rest to Sri Choudhury in the Rest house.

Before leaving we asked for some tea and biscuit and discussed the arrangement for the night. The staff had started cooking their dinner; I suddenly heard a loud clanking of the chain tied to Agasthi's hind legs. I told Sri Choudhury that, the tusker has got loose. He did not believe. I could faintly see him speeding away through paddy fields in the faint moon light. All the staff got up and followed. I and Sri B.C.Prusty, the IFS probationer, who later headed the Tiger Project was close to Agasthi while Sri Choudhury loaded M-99 in his pistol. Field bunds after bunds had to be negotiated one after the other. It was difficult to judge their height in poor light. The batteries of torches had been partly discharged and the visibility was poor. He was very fast. We all fell, rolled, tore our dresses, bruised and followed him.

Sri Choudhury got him rather at a very close distance and fired the dart. But it was difficult to judge the distance. As a result it was too close for the given charge to work effectively. Instead of the drug getting in to his body, it was pushed out and a drop fell on the face of Prusty as he was closest to the tusker. He returned to me and said, sir, I cannot see and my mouth is bitter. I could guess what has happened. By the time the person with M. 50-50 the antidote which was with Sri Choudhury reaches it would be quite late. We were close to a village. We saw some water flowing out of the hand operated village tube well. We initially washed his face with the water and then poured water from the tube well to dilute the drug. M 50-50 was injected ten minutes after. But the water had already washed off the drug and reduced its effect. We thanked God that Prusty was saved. This is a very strong drug, one drop of which could be fatal for man. There have been cases in other countries, where careless handling of the drug had resulted in fatalities.

We continued our chase through more and more of fields. It was tough. Everyone was very tired and hungry. Sri Choudhury's face was wet with perspiration. He was oldest of the lot in his 57th year. But he never stayed back. We were overhearing the staff resenting this operation from a distance. They were fatigued. This chase continued down south for about sixteen kilometers and Agasthi's distance from us was increasing till the Berhampur-Aska road was reached. Even at that hour at about 10.30 the road was busy with vehicles going in either direction. To go to Kerandimal forest, he was required to cross this road. He could not do that due to heavy traffic and had to slow down. We knew that this was our last opportunity to dart him. Sri Choudhury had already loaded the pistol and with torch light focused on his rump, he aimed and fired. He ran for about fifty meters and fell on a field. We knew that there was no tree to tie him up. There was a small culvert nearby. We conferred and decided to tie him to a log of wood which will be held by both the retaining walls of the culvert. People were sent to the saw mills to procure a stout 4 m. long Sal log. His legs were tied to very strong railway safety chain that was used to pull railway wagons with U-bolts. Then a sisal rope was tied to the chain. This in turn was passed under the culvert and tied to a very stout log, kept on the other side of the road. He was injected with the antidote. But we saw no indication of his revival. The pulse was low. We prayed 'God' for his early revival. His prolonged run to escape had its effect. It was the slowest recovery. It was at around 1.30 a.m. when he showed signs of reviving and tried to get up around 2.00 a.m. We were relieved and decided to leave him alone for some food and little rest for us to come back early in the morning to shift him to a proper place for tying as there was neither shade nor a large tree here. The road also could not be used by people if he is kept there. It was difficult to get some food for all of us at that hour. We searched and located a *Dhaba*, the Indian version of a motel mainly for truck drivers, which served us some *roti* and curry. We slept with our field dresses on. Sleep came to me in a minute and I slept till I saw Sri Choudhury on my bedside next morning calling "Saroj", holding a cup of coffee and few pieces of 'coconut crunches' biscuits, his favorite munch. I sprang up from my bed and looked at my watch. It was already six. In few minutes I was at the wheel of the jeep, after a quick breakfast and sped towards the spot that was about 7 km. from the Rest House. It was a scene to watch on the feeder road, near which Agasthi was tied to the culvert. He just went up the road blocking this narrow road completely. He had still not overcome the sedation of previous night and was standing still. Thousands of people had gathered by then and vehicles, bullock carts and rickshaws stood in long lines on either side of the elephant. We knew, he had to be shifted immediately away from the road to clear the road for free movement of vehicles. We scouted for a suitable location. A large banyan tree was about couple of hundred meters away from the culvert. It was quite a good spot as it had shade, a flat cultivated land with a large tank about 3-4 hundred meters away deep enough for an elephant to bathe. We decided the shift him there within the village limits of Ratanpur. It was quite risky to shift him as in the process, he could escape. We had to act fast. We attached *Sisal* rope to the chain on his hind legs though a noose and tied with a long sisal rope to the tree trunk while still keeping the rope intact around the log. About 200 people including forest staff took part is the pulling process, while tightening the rope around the tree. Some pushing was done from behind. He inched forward till he was only 10 meters from the tree. He was securely tied and given tree fodder, banana and water. We set up a camp there and the staff from different ranges took turns to maintain vigil. The problem of thousands of people coming to see him was to be handled properly. We requested police help. Local people composed songs and came to sing with *'mridangs'*, harmoniums, cymbals and other traditional folk instruments. I stayed on there on the open ground with loaded guns for the safely of people. However to train him was quite a difficult proposition. Orissa had no trainer left as there had been no elephant capture after 1946. Sri Choudhury decided to request Sri S. Debroy, then Field Director, Manas Tiger Reserve, Assam for a trainer. We also asked Nandankanan to send their two cow elephants and the elephant 'Laxmi' belonging to Lord Jagannath, the most revered deity of Odias world wide located at Puri. But all of them were scared of going close to him as he was a very hefty and strong animal and slight push sent them screaming and running in pain. Laxmi who was quite old, almost shivered and avoided going close to him as he was very healthy and robust tusker. I also felt that she was too weak to be taken close to him. However the Nandankanan elephants were needed to be kept for handling any difficult unforeseen situation.

Agasthi kept on pulling hard and in the process injured himself as the chains were slowly eating in to his skin. This was further worsening due to his urine. We kept on spraying antiseptics and fly repellants. He could understand this move and kept showing his wounds to us and cooperated. Sri Choudhury had been to Nilgiris in Southern India for some official work. We waited for him to sedate or immobilize him for proper treatment as his maggoted wounds needed to be dressed and injected with long acting antibiotics. This helped him recover.

Agasthi being trained. Photographed by Author

In the meantime Sri Jatin Rava, the master trainer along with an assistant reached the site from Assam to help train the tusker. Agasthi was placed between two stout Sal logs and all his four legs were tied with jute fiber ropes almost going round half of all the four leg surfaces with little scope for moving. This fiber is much softer than other materials. The training started with '*Tantrik Puja*' as is done in Assam with animal (male poultry bird called '*ganja*' in Odia) sacrifice. They started fire, beating of drums, massaging with paddy straw, singing, patting and finally rewarding with sugarcane pieces etc when he obeyed orders. He was fed and bathed on the spot. He slept standing there too. But after few days he started taking commands. After about a fortnight, he was taken for bath with other elephants and later taken alone with only *Mahouts* guiding him.

When it was felt that he can now be controlled with relative ease, we decided to take him to Nandankanan. The road journey was meticulously planned. The camps were carefully planned about 20 kms away from each other and their sites were selected in advance. Two vehicles with camping equipments also followed him while two tame elephants moved on his right on the National Highway (N.H-No.5). We all followed him on foot for the first two days. He behaved quite well and moved for 4 to 5 hours every day. We later learnt that this is the first ever capture and training of an Asian elephant through tranquilization anywhere in the world.

The first day's march was quite critical and we all kept our fingers crossed and avoided the main road as much as possible. Ultimately there was no escape. He had to be taken through the highway. Initially he reacted to the never-ending stream of vehicles. He paused and went down the road and was brought back by the *Mahouts* with lot of coxing. But with time he got used to it. At this juncture the confidence of the *Mahout* and his confidence on his *Mahout* was very important as an elephant can face any obstacle if he trusts his master. The master in turn has to be caring and instill confidence in him. By the second day he had reached and camped at Ganjam. But on the 4th day a nice camping site in a mango grove at Khallikot was reached and it was decided to stay there for some days to rest the animal as well as Mahouts and other staff who were walking daily.

I reached this place one evening on the 4th, May, 1982 to see how Agasthi is and when to start the 2nd phase of the journey towards Nandankanan. It was evening. And eerie silence hand descended on the scene except for braking of branches by the three elephants tied to the 3 mango trees. As we came close, the staff came and conveyed to me half sobbing that Sri Saroj Raj Choudhury is no more. They have got the news over their portable radio, though I did not know anything as I came from the forest tour. He died at Jashipur that morning of a massive heart attack while having his breakfast. A legend had passed away. Many people said that the tiring work of capturing the tusker was too much for this 57 years old forester, who knew forest and wildlife of this country perhaps more intimately than all other persons of his time. His empathy for wild animals knew no bounds. He was awarded Padmashree, a national award for his dedicated service to this cause after his death. This was small recognition for his lifetime of dedicated service of introducing training in systematic wildlife management in the country and developing census technique for tigers and leopards. His meticulous research work on Khairi, the tigress who stayed with him and his very daring cousin Ms. Nihar in Jashipur had thrown light on many unknown aspects of tiger behaviour. She (Khairi) had died a year back of rabies leaving him and her foster mother highly depressed. It was difficult for them to overcome the loss. In my mind I saluted this hero and asked the staff to get ready to move to Bhubaneswar with Agasthi as there was none to look to incase of any problem. The staff had not cooked their food, mourning the loss. I persuaded them to cook and take their dinner.

Agasthi reached Nandankanan on 13th, May, 1982 and stayed with other cow elephants and little calves blind Laxmi and Ganesh with an injured hind leg. He slowly started taking people on elephant rides.

I followed him to Nandankanan as its director in February, 83. Agasthi continued to stay in the park. He was quite hale and hearty for first few years of his stay. But his health failed gradually. When none of the medications worked and wounds did not heal, we tested his blood for sugar content and found him afflicted by diabetes. We knew the treatment for an elephant shall be quite expensive, but continued treatment. His ordeal continued till he breathed his last several years after his capture. He almost lived a full life saved from premature death by firing.

This adorable tusker had taught a lot of lessons to the forest staff and others who got associated with his capture, training, care and medications. A gentleman of a tusker, who never harmed anybody despite provocations, except a mild playful push to me with his trunk, when I withheld few bananas from him, will be remembered as long as I live.

May his soul rest in peace!

(The detailed article on the capture and training by Sri Choudhury was published in Hornbill (BNHS), 1982(3), July-September: 25-29 and reprinted in 'Elephants in Similipal(STR) in2001

———————— ✦✦✦✦✦ ————————

19

KANAN – THE LONELY TIGRESS

It was a morning as usual in the 8-year-old zoo, Nandankanan, named so after the 'heavenly garden of gods', on the outskirts of Bhubaneswar, the newly planned capital city of Odisha'. Everybody was much exited to see the huge tiger, Pradeep housed for the first time in an open air moated enclosure on the previous day.

It was a chilly January morning in 1967. The mist was yet to lift and due drops shone like pearls on the grasses and leaves as the early morning sunlight filtered through the vegetation of this zoo carved out of a natural forest. The cleaning staff went out to sweep the road next to this open air exhibit on the 5th, January, where the visitors could see the animal from the road, while the lone tiger moved inside the paddock shaded with indigenous trees, canes and bamboo clumps. But to their utter surprise they saw two tigers instead of one released there on the previous day.

'Kanan' jumping into the enclosure.

It was on the 4th of January evening the parapet made of laterite blocks separating the visitors from the paddock (the open space provided for movement of animals)used by the tiger was just plastered The backside of this paddock was protected with 5.5m high chain link mesh fence. Both of them were growling in rage and had injury on their body with gush of cuts. Sri Saroj Raj Choudhury, the legendary wildlifer, who as Wildlife Conservation Officer looked after the fledgling park, Dr Acharjyo, the Veterenary Surgeon, Sri Ghanshyam Nayak, the ACF, Sri Bhajaram Jena, Range Officer and all other staff were all pleasantly surprised to see this lovely animal who had come to the enclosure and sacrificed her freedom for the sake of companionship. As this was a unique case anywhere in the world, international press covered the incident. So much so a subsequent issue of 'National Geographic' reported the incident. It was correlated with the previous sightings of a tigress in different parts of the zoo which was contiguous to the Chandaka Forest, which was earlier famous for its good population and hunting of tigers by *shikaris* like Sri Gadadhar Ray, a famous *shikar* (hunting) story writer of the State. Her pug marks were also seen at several places in the park, which had no compound wall then. It was very clear that this tigress had jumped in to this beautiful enclosure, as there was no formidable barrier to be crossed to enter in to the exhibit. Only two and half feet of parapet wall had to be climbed and then jump down the wall of about sixteen feet. This was no problem for a large powerful cat like tiger and she had done this taking advantage of the darkness. She had slid down the newly plastered parapet damaging the plaster with her weight. It was clear that she was in estrous and during this time females in the wild come close to their male mates, though during the rest of the time they confine themselves to their respective territory which is demarcated with marking fluid, called pheromone sprayed from the hind parts of a tiger on shrubs, trees, logs, boulders and bushes. They closely guard their territory marked with 'pheromone' and do not loose time to launch an attack on any intruder if not in 'estrous,' a stage of sexual high, when mating does take place. Cases of tigers killing the intruders even of opposite sex, straying in to their territory in other times is not uncommon.

It was later established that she was the lone tigress left in the famous Chandaka Forest, spared by licensed *shikaris* and poachers. The shifting of capital city of Orissa from Cuttack to Bhubaneswar had already depleted the forest growth and brought many armed people to the area. The thin forest growth had hardly left any cover for the large cats who had fallen prey to poachers' bullet along with many other species like Leopard, Samber, Cheetal, Gaur, mouse dear, barking dear, peafowl and sometimes even elephants. It was also famous for its large population of snakes on which thrived a colony of snake charmers called '*Kela*' in Padmakesharipur near Patia. She created international zoo history, being first tigress to have left wilderness and chosen captivity. She was christened 'Kanan' after the name of Nandankanan, the zoo.

What she never knew was that her decision to jump the parapet was irreversible, as it was impossible to escape from the enclosure. She strongly resented her captivity and attacked Pradeep quite often. They were separated to prevent conflict, which could have been fatal to any of them. Of course Pradeep created history among all tigers in captivity in the country to have the largest progeny, which has been distributed all over the country. Though Kanan stayed in captivity in the park till her death for long eleven years upto1978, she had refused to mate.

The mark on the cement mortar is still preserved as a historical land mark and shown to visitors for more than 3 decades now. A board marks the place where this event took place, which is repeatedly shown to the tourist groups by the tourist guides.

This is one of the sad stories of decimation of this majestic feline not in the state but also in the entire country. Various factors like habitat loss, fragmentation, poaching for hides and other tiger parts, much in demand outside the country and declining pray base have contributed to its decline to less than two thousand from an estimated forty thousand in the early part of last century. Let us all work together to save this beautiful animal and its pristine habitats from the threshold of extinction.

This type of an incident has also been repeated in the same zoo recently, when a male tiger has travelled about 200 kilometers from a Tiger Reserve and has become captive after moving in the zoo premises and surrounding forests for several days. There appears to be no tiger of breeding age left in that reserve, though there is excellent prey base and cover for a good population of tigers.

───────── ᛫᛫✦✦✦᛫᛫ ─────────

20

FILMING BLACK BUCKS

It was a winter afternoon in 1979 and as the sun was to set quite early we were in a great hurry to make a TV film for Cuttack Doordarshan on black bucks, the antelopes whose males turn jet black with white under belly as they grow up. Dr. P.K. Mohapatra a very devoted TV producer was with his team of technical personnel with heavy equipments, as present day the sleek TV cameras complete with sound recording system had not made their entry in to TV studios. The slim bodied athletic animals drifted away from us, took to their feet and leaped across field bunds in almost horizontal gallops unique to the species. There were almost 40 to 50 of them while few adult males at a distance looked on.

As the folk lore goes, these antelopes rather strange to this country-side were first spotted in the area after a long seven years of famine in the middle of nineteenth century and after their arrival in this tract clouds opened up and there was good rain, which broke the drought spell and bumper crop harvest followed.

After that the villagers of Bhetnoi in southern Odisha district of Ganjam and neighboring group of villages started protecting these animals and rather revered them. They were so familiar to the local people that when they work in the field with their usual *'dhoti'* or *'gamchha'* they do come very close. They sometimes come into the villages when food is scarce in the fields and take cattle feed from the troughs, kept for cows.

The villagers here are so protective of these animals that it is said that an all powerful British Collector was captured by the villagers and tied to the tree for poaching a black buck is early twentieth century and they refused to set him free until he was forced pay a hefty fine for the crime and the carcass was buried. There are many incidents of unscrupulous poachers attempting to poach and getting caught and punished.

It is through their efforts the species has been saved in the area and their number is on the rise.

As this species normally grazes on very tender grasses in absolutely open landscapes like Rajasthan and Gujarat, it inhabits the open crop fields of this tract and grazes on tender seedlings of different serials and legumes here. Requirement of water for the black bucks is minimal, which is met mostly from the vegetation it ingested. Tree lands are avoided by the species. As a result the crop fields in the vast plains here are often depredated by herds of those beautiful creatures when any crop is young. But, no villager harms any animal. Rather, orphaned young ones are seen being nursed by villagers.

But it was a different case with us. We wanted to shoot with our camera to show the outside world that wildlife can be saved in the country with active support of the local people.

But we were all in western clothes. We were at our wits end. Dr. Mohapatra had taken lot of trouble to travel to this area for the film for which I had written the script. Those days TV films were shot in a large cameras using film spools and sound was recorded in a separate recorder. The pictures were in black and white.

Villagers and even the passersby on this district road were curious. Many used to pass through this road regularly, without noticing these animals and often discarded them as herds of goats. Finally the villagers came to our rescue and told us to don their farming attire and then go closer. Even some volunteered with their clothes. Without losing time the producer and his crew changed to rural attire with bare upper body and turbans as head gear and proceeded in to the field. Lo and behold an excellent shooting session continued till the fading late afternoon light permitted. Dr. Mohapatra appeared very satisfied.

Filming the Blackbucks.

These were the main visuals for the film. But it has to be given the right introduction so that it falls into a storyline and gives the right massage.

We shifted to my official residence of Divisional Forest Officer, Bhanjanagar a massive British day bungalow standing on the center of a nine acre campus. With mud walls of about two feet (60 cum) thick, the single storey mansion towered over modern three – storied buildings and had roof of thick paddy straw thatch over a timber superstructure. Rooms were so large that one could lay a full sized badminton court in its drawing room.

There was good mango grove with select varieties of mango trees, large kitchen garden and two gates for coming in and going out. It had a long row of houses attached, which, as I learnt was meant to house camp followers of the officer occupying the house few decades back, when touring in the forest was done on foot or on horseback. They were deputed by village head men by rotation to go to the forest camps as advance parties to carry camping equipments and pitch tents so that the officer can follow and stay there. Leaf huts were made for housing subordinates and labour force. Of course this was a practice in the British days. As this southern district was part of the erstwhile Madras Presidency, I learnt that the Governor of Madras while on tour to this far flung northern corner of his presidency used to stay in this bungalow till 1926.

Coming back to the black buck film, we used my residential office room where a child that is my eldest daughter 'Nipa' was filmed going through the world map then India map and further to Odisha and finally to Ganjam, zooming onto Bhetanoi and see black bucks leaping in their majestic forms in order to establish a story line. I was told by Doordarshan by which name the first TV channel is known, that not only the film was a great success, but it won a prize in a Japanese TV competition. Unfortunately I have not been able to see the film as those days we did not have a TV in our house and the range of TV station would not cover my headquarters. Thanks to the protection provided by the local people their number is on the rise and their territory is spreading. They are seen from north of Karsing into Nayagarh district and Buguda area, near Kabisuryanagar and Krushnagiri. Of course there is also a small population in the coastal sandy stretches of Ganjam and Puri districts. Though a census conducted during my time in 1980 put their number at 480, it is learnt that it has crossed two thousand now and the spread of their occurrence has more than doubled. But the coastal population has virtually vanished perhaps due to Casuarina and cashewnut plantations raised as a safeguard against coastal cyclones. Efforts are underway to reintroduce them there in large clearings.

21

PLUNDER OF PANDRIPADA FOREST

The sun was yet to appear in the eastern horizon on this summer morning. I was stretching myself on a camp cot in front of the Forest Guard shed is this small hamlet about 3 km from Kodala after a very busy night without any sleep. The F.G. shed was holding number of persons arrested for forest offences during the night. And village women made their noisy presence felt as they were going towards the forest to fetch fuel wood for their hearth.

This was an operation perhaps first of its kind in Odisha by the Forest Department. I had joined the Ghumusar South Division as its Divisional Forest Officer few months back. I had learnt that this area is notorious for its theft of timber from the forests of Pandripada, also known as Singhasani forest after the name of the deity located in the heart of this forest patch. Local forest staff and police were scared of these timber smugglers, who were very daring and would not hesitate to lethally attack anybody coming on their way.

I considered this as my very first challenge and decided on taking them head on. But, for doing that sufficient intelligence regarding their time of visit, number of persons in the group, involvement or support of our own staff, type of weapon they carry etc was absolutely essential for planning an offensive. I decided to do this intelligence gathering myself.

For the purpose of maintaining secrecy I took a Mahindra Jeep from another division and took a young Forest Ranger probationer totally new to the area with me. I carried packed lunch for both of us and proceeded to the area devastated by tree felling. It appeared that they picked up all sound trees, felled them and took the button logs leaving the upper parts and branches on the site. The entire area from where trees were felled looked like an extensive grave yard. I saw the Forest Guards hut nearby.

Instead of talking to any forest staff, I called few villagers who appeared to be quite active and enjoyed respect from others. Took them aside and while talking on different aspect of their day to day life casually asked about the timber smuggling. They were quite frank as they did not know who I was. They told me that people from a village close to Kodala do usually come in groups of about hundred or so persons with buffalo carts up through a tortuous cart track in the morning. Fell and log the trees, while some of them cook their food. After all logging is completed; they load them by evening and leave after an evening meal. They buy young buffaloes every year and sell off the older ones, as they become unserviceable in the next season due to heavy load they are made to carry after intoxicating them with country liquor.

I also asked about the role of the local forest staff. They informed me that they were simply scared of facing them and either avoid the site completely or stay indoors.

Then I called one of them who was forthcoming with all information to a little secluded place and introduced myself as the new DFO. He was surprised that there was no forest staff with me. I told him since these smugglers almost stay for 10 hours at the site, would it be possible for them to inform me and how much time they would take to reach Bhanjanagar. Those days in 1979 there no proper telephone connectivity, mobile phones were yet to appear in the scene, forest department except Similipal Tiger Reserve, did not have any wireless (VHF) for internal communication. He said that they can cycle down to Bhanjanagar through a short cut route and reach is 3 hours. I told him that he and his comparison shall be rewarded and due secrecy shall be maintained regarding their identity. We had a *darshan* (paying obeisance) of the deity Singhasini, a local Hindu goddess and returned back to Bhanjanagar. Days and months passed after this visit.

It was on the 3rd, May 1979 at about 11.00 am when I was holding my monthly divisional meeting with Range Officers, someone peeped through the door curtains and tried to open it 3-4 times to attract my attention. Initially I was irritated as to why someone is trying to disturb us. Suddenly the person I met in Singhasini flashed in my mind and I could recognize that this is that person.

I abruptly suspended the meeting for 15 minutes and called him in. The information he gave me was spine chilling. He told me that about 100 people have come with more than 30 carts and have settled down for cooking their meals and felling trees. They may leave the place after evening.

I knew neither we had the man power nor fire power to face so many well built persons with lethal weapons, dreaded even by police. I asked him as to which was the best place to intercept them. He said, "As they go down the slope they shall pass through an old mango tree, where the track is very narrow. And because of heavy load, some of them have to help each cart to come down and as such 3-4 carts shall come together to the place and the people go back to help others." This was enough information.

I called back all Range Officers and asked them to collect 60 strong bamboo sticks and 12, 5-cell new torches and come back after lunch. We also got some unserviceable guns in the office which were also cleaned up. I talked to all other DFOs and Divisional Manager, OFDC located at Bhanjanagar. Requested them to spare all their jeeps and uniformed manpower including orderly and office peons they can spare. To my surprise no one hesitated. We had 40 people with us and 7 vehicles. My attempt to contact Superintendent of Police and Collector located at Chatrapur was in vain as phone lines were not in order. Even Divisional Manager of Forest Corporation at Berhampur could not be contacted. But I felt it essential to keep the district administration informed before carrying out such a daring operation with unarmed forest staff at the dead of night.

I called my ACF and Range Officers back to the meeting and gave them final briefing as I cannot meet them again before the operation. We decided that all of them should proceed to Buguda, the other range headquarter of my division and take dinner there, which would be kept ready before they arrive. All jeeps except one would have its number plate displaying its identity smeared with mud. They will pass through Kodala with their side and back flaps closed at an interval of 15 minutes each. But the last one with number plates clear and flaps open with the ACF and Range Officer Kodala should go to the Police Station and give them a written request for help and proceed with or without help. This was done, as I knew that the smugglers keep people at Kodala with two wheelers to watch movement of forest staff, who proceed to inform them when there is suspicious movement of forest or police personnel.

I myself proceeded via Berhampur to Chatrapur to meet the Collector and Superintendent of Police and take an additional vehicle from the Divisional Manager of the forest corporation, Berhampur. I got a vehicle from Berhampur and some more forest staff. The Collector was absent but the S.P. had just returned from tour. His first reaction was I should abandon this operation as it is too risky. I told him that it is too late now to call off the move as the staff must have reached the site. If possible he should lend me some force. He was very reluctant, but had to write to the Inspector-in-Charge of the force deployed at Khallikote for next day's Panchayat Election. He told that he can spare half a section of armed force of 5 men if transport is provided by the Forest Department., but they have to return for their duty in the morning. I agreed and proceeded. The Kodala Police also accompanied, though very reluctantly.

We decided to form a horse shoe pattern formation around the spot, keeping the entry free and when one group of carts reach the appointed spot and staff standing in formation all around to flash torches on their eyes and over power them before they could react and take them to Forest Guard's hut about 1 km away where I positioned myself. They were held there under close watch. The carts would be driven by another group of people recruited from another village.

The first group of three carts came to our net at around mid night. By early morning all 33 carts were seized and about 70 persons arrested leaving children who accompanied elders.

As early morning sun rays were filtering through the foliage, a procession of carts, arrested persons and forest vehicles started for Kodala, where there was a judicial court and a sub-jail. Everyone was hungry.

I asked our staff to prepare *'Suji halwa'*, a local quick to prepare sweet snack, for everyone for breakfast as anything else was cumbersome and time consuming to prepare.

As I was taking my breakfast of *halwa* Sri Ramakrishna Patnaik, local Member of Legislative Assembly who was also a senior Minister in the state earlier and even later came to the Rest House and talked to me about the operation. He said, "I came for something else, but having seen the effort all of you have put in, I shall not interfere in your activity."

All timbers were measured, hammer marked and recorded and loaded to 10 trucks and sent to Buguda along with the carts after dismantling them. The buffaloes were given in *zima* (safe custody) of the relatives of the accused persons. The accused persons were produced before the Magistrate when office opened and remanded to custody. There was such a crowd to see the arrested persons, carts, buffaloes and timber that temporary tea stalls opened up in front of the court.

Few days after this we raided the village to unearth the timber stolen earlier. Of course this time with good support from the police. I incidentally had an 'umpire stick' which was perhaps used by cricket umpires of those days, made in Kerala of rose wood. As I was going to dumps suspected to have timber, I used that stick to strike the dumps to find out if there was loose earth. People started talking that this forest officer is carrying a machine that detects hidden timber. People stopped hiding them and even few threw them in the open. We came up with a huge seizure.

The humiliation of confrontation and arrest by hurriedly gathered unarmed forest staff without any exposure to any such operation, of so many people was too much for their ego as even the armed and organized police was scared to confront these hardened smugglers even during day time. I learnt that, most of notorious smugglers left their village for labor work in Assam, a north eastern state. I must give credit to the staff of my division and those from other divisions for their bravery of carrying out this daring operation, though they had never been exposed to any such in the past and upheld prestige of the department, despite risk of being overpowered. They reposed full faith in me. After this incident, I stayed for 3years in that division and did not face any such organized illicit removal.

The Deputy Inspector General, a regional police head, in his crime meeting analyzed this operation in great detail and attributed its success to 'element of surprise' of the operation and they felt that any slip off could have been disastrous for these unarmed personnel.

••••••••

22

THE LAST KHEDA

As a little kid I was staying in Keonjhar or better known as Keonjhar Garh or Kendujhar Garh those days, '*Garh*' or '*Gada*' meaning the capital of a princely state then known as '*Gadjat*' or '*Garhjat*'. My father was a forester who was holding post of DFO, Sadar, in that state, now Keonjhar district. The state had 3 Divisional Forest Officers, other two were located at Anandpur and Champua. The state's forest department was headed by a Chief Forest Officer, who usually used to be a British Officer, before Indian foresters took over.

It was winter months when I found that some captive elephants, with *gaddis* tied on their backs, were brought into large compound of our official residence with their *mahauts* and helpers. Father and others told that they had come from different princely states (*gadjats*) for *Khedda* operation. I had no idea what does a *Khedda* mean. But I was quite fascinated to see the captive elephants and their activities and used to spend quite some time in observing them eating, bathing and taking human commands, in language alien to me. Then, after some days the elephants were gone making me and my siblings sad and my father also left home for quite a few days and it was said that he had gone for the *'Khedda'*.

Later on when I joined forest service and wildlife conservation became my passion; I came to know that that was the last *Khedda* ever held in Odisha and the year was 1946. Of course at that point of time the state was not a part of the Orissa province and a king ruled it like 22 others which merged in1948. Only Mayurbhanj merged in 1949. A stone plaque stands now at a place some distance away from present National Highway No. 6 indicating the date and place where that *Khedda* operation was carried out. Perhaps that was closer to the old Atharabanki, a narrow, single lane winding road that only allowed movement of very small buses, which were too few in numbers those days. Not only Keonjhar, states like Mayurbhanj, Bamra, Narasinghpur and Pallahada etc organized *Khedda* to capture elephants as they were badly needed those days for travelling into the forest areas or inaccessible areas by the *Rajas* and their officers for logging, *shikar*, inspection and other purposes. Mechanized vehicles were too few in number and very few tracts were connected though motorable roads. The kings of different states in Odisha and neighboring areas used to send their captive trained elephants when *Khedda* operations were carried out in any state and used to share elephants captured in the operation. Some of them are known to be sold out. Dignitaries were also invited from other states or other parts of the country to watch the operation. Those days Odisha had six districts directly administered by the British and 24 princely states. 23 out of them used to be under control of Political Agent of Eastern States Agency with headquarters at Raipur. Incidentally a very sincere, hard working and competent British forester named Dr. H.F. Mooney used to be the Forest Advisor of this Agency. He trekked through most forests in these inhospitable tracts for months and wrote vivid accounts of his visits. He is responsible for first working plans for forests of many of these states, which were outcome of his visits to these forests. He was an excellent botanist and had his contribution to the Flora of Bihar and Orissa, which is a monumental work.

As the *Khedda* of Odisha, earlier named as Kalinga, which named its king as Gajapati was soon vanishing from the public memory, I as the Chief Wildlife Warden had requested Dr U.N. Dev, a former prince himself and an ornithologist of repute to dig out the history of elephant capture from different states. His report indicated that not only *Khedaa,* two other methods namely *'phasa'*, meaning 'noose' and *'topa or khanda'* meaning 'pit' were also practiced in Odisha, though to a lesser extent.

In *Khedda* method, a forested valley with good number of wild elephants was first selected and surrounded with people camping in leaf huts specially erected for the purpose, equipped with fire crackers, burning fires, drums and tin cans etc to create sound for scaring the elephants. A rectangular stockade called *'girda'* made of stout Sal logs was built with a funnel shaped entry. The *'girda'* had a stout drop gate made of Sal poles fixed with pointed large wooden pegs, pointing inwards. The entry path was stocked with items like banana plants, paddy rolled in paddy straw bundles etc loved by elephants. Once the contrivance was ready, the people surrounding the valley would beat drums, tin cans, shout, make fires and burst crackers to drive elephants to the funnel and then lured by eatables the herd would gradually move towards the *'girda'* protected by people and trained elephants. Once sufficient number required by the concerned states get into the *girda*, the drop gate rope would be cut by people perched on trees. Once entrapped, commotion would start among the elephants, who would try to dash against the gate. But the stout wooden spikes would deter them.

After a while they would reconcile to their fate and become calm. In few days in captivity without sufficient food, they would become weaker. Then domestic *'kumki'* elephants would be introduced into the stockade. Each captured elephant would be tied with stout ropes by the *'mahauts'* tied to under belly of *kumkies* and led out of the 'girda' to pre-determined places where training would start. The training which is done in 'kraals' made of solid timber would last between one to three months. After this the elephants would be put to use in that state or given to other states or sold.

Besides *'khedda'* Odisha practiced capture by pit method by digging deep pits on the elephant track and covering it with freshly cut branches with foliage. When unsuspecting elephants would pass over them, they would fall into them and would not be able be come out on their own. Then a ramp would be made and the elephant would be tied with stout ropes and laid outside the pit through the ramp with help of captive elephants and similar training would follow. This method was discouraged due to injuries caused to most elephants resulting in death of few. As far as my information goes, the last such operation was organized in Raygada area of South Odisha.

Similarly, the 'noose' method adopted in the state was different from *'mela shikar'* of Assam. In this case a noose with very large opening would be made with stout rope hanging from 2 stout trees located on either side of elephant track. When any elephant would pass through this, it would get entangled with the noose which would tighten as the pachyderm pulled with its full strength and the animal would not be able to move away. Then the process of securing and training would be similar as in earlier cases. This method also had very limited acceptance as it was very site specific and captures used to be very few.

As use of elephant in logging and tours to interiors stopped after independence and with merger of princely states in 1948, due to introduction of jeeps and gradual opening of forest roads, capture of elephants using any method was stopped.

Use of chemical immobilization as a capture technique for problematic, sick or injured animals started from 1982 with capture of a tusker, Agasthi in Ganjam by late Saroj Raj Choudhury. He was trained by trainers from Assam. Few more such cases followed and are continuing till date particularly for capture of problem or injured animals.

The Orissa District Gazetteers of Mayurbhanj published in 1967 indicates that the last *khedda* of Mayurbhanj was held in 1938. Though it says that kheddas were a very regular feature in the state and occurred every few years and that catching of elephants was a favourite sport of princes for many centuries; very few records are available.

There is a brief description of Khedda method mentioned in it which goes as follows:

Khedda operations used to be in the nature of festivities to which VIPs were invited. After the elephants were located in forest, these used to be surrounded by watchers and at the end there used to be a fortified enclosure called 'stockade' with an entrance. The elephants were attracted into the enclosure by their favourite food, paddy and banana plants. Immediately after the herd entered, a strong door with nails sticking out was dropped to close it. There used to be a double line of fortification with either a moat surrounding the stockade or a second line of fence with the intervening space filled with logs or woods placed horizontally.

The few records of Mayurbhanj Kheda mentioned in the gazetteer are:

1870-71	200 elephants were caught.
1910	Elephants caught, as witnessed by the Chief Editor. (During the 40 intervening years there must have been Kheda operations, but no record exists).
1931-32	Kheda operations were held at Chekamara but details are not available. The Maharaja of Nikaneer, Rajas of Nilgiri and of Puri attended the operations.

| 1933-34 | 20 elephants caught at a cost of Rs.12,076 at Khandabuda. The Maharaja of Jaipur and Panna witnessed the Kheda operations. |
| 1937-38 | 15 elephants caught at a cost of Rs.20,561 at a place 16 miles away from Baripada town. |

It was also mentioned that ruins of large stockades at Pragana, Arpata, Chilma and Similipal and small stockades at Puruna Baripada and Orachandabila were available till 1932.

Maharaja Krushna chandra caught elephants in Ahari Jungle in Banahari Pragana and Maharaja Sri Rama chandra caught a large number at Dengam, Jaypur, Pithabata, Chekamara and Mangarh jungles. Maharaja Purna chandra caught elephants at Unkura in 1932. Elephants were caught at Champagarh by Maharaja Pratap Chandra.

In 1943 a single elephant was caught in trap. Strong ropes were laid and a man sat on top of a tree. As the elephant touched the trap a light went up and the man pulled the ropes. The elephant was caught. Since then there has been no catching of elephants. That was perhaps the last capture of any elephant in Mayurbhanj. The Mayurbhanj state merged with the Indian Union in 1949 and the course of management of Similipal became different.

As *Kheddas* of Mysore, which were known as 'river drive kheddas' on the banks of Kabini continued much after our independence, perhaps till late sixties, they are still etched in peoples' memory and are well known as they are well documented. But, our kheddas in Odisha have all but forgotten and the traditional *'Mahunta'* or 'Mahaut' families in states like Mayurbhanj, Keonjhar, Boudh and Deogarh etc have forgotten the skill practiced by their fore fathers. Odisha state has no private elephants left and all captive elephants belong to the state forest department.

Though around 2,000 wild elephants still live in the state, the depletion their habitats, loss of migratory safe corridors etc due to various anthropogenic causes have resulted in their wandering out of their natural habitat in to paddy fields, villages and even into the towns and cities and they come in to conflict with people resulting in loss of property and lives. This has also triggered retaliatory killing of elephants besides electrocution and other accidents. It is high time that we must do everything possible to save this magnificent species.

23

TESTING OVERHAULED BOULA

It was a rain soaked July late afternoon in the office of Mangrove Wildlife Division at Rajnagar. The River Brahmani was flooded and was threatening to breach its embankments. As usual, I was reviewing progress of different works in the division and sorting out problems faced in the field. The day was witnessing highest flood levels in Brahmani River and flood waters almost touched the brim of the river embankment. Sri Sanjiv Kumar Chadha who was the Divisional Forest Officer was under orders of transfer and the DFO, designate Sri Asish Mohapatra was with me to have a firsthand exposure to the problems of the division when he talks to Sanjiv. As we were about to leave Rajnagar the DFO told me that the main motor launch of the Division named 'Boula', after the local name of estuarine crocodile has been completely overhauled as I told him and is lying in Hansua, a very deep tidal river close to the office. I was eager to see it as that was our main life line and was quite comfortable and stable. Though we wanted to leave in order to be safe from the swelling river water, I could not resist my temptation of seeing the boat fully overhauled. We rushed to the river bank and boarded the boat and inspected its interiors. It was very good work done. I asked Sanjiv as to whether the engine and other moving parts have been attended to. As he replied in affirmative, I asked the Launch Driver to start the boat and take us on a small round. He immediately started the engine and we were off from the shore of this very deep swelling tidal river infested with crocodiles. We had just reached the mid-stream, when the gears stopped functioning. We were freely floating and drifting towards a bridge located downstream. Everyone was scared at the prospect to hilting the pier of the bridge at very high speed which may result in the boat disintegrating to pieces. If we escape that we shall be drifting towards the sea and the fast river current will enhance the boat's velocity. Not knowing what to do, everyone panicked. But an old man who was a part of the launch crew without anyone noticing him tied a long piece of rope, which was lying on the deck to his waist and jumped into the water and started swimming ashore without any attention to his personal safety. His jump propelled the boat towards the shore and as he hit mud, which is common in tidal rivers of Bhitarkanika, he started pulling the boat towards the shore.

His presence of mind and courage saved all of us as all of us heaved a sigh of relief. I indeed admire the dedication, tenacity and courage of the field staff of this division who work relentlessly in very difficult conditions of this national park any time during day or night without bothering about their personal comforts. Any praise for these underpaid staff will be simply inadequate.

***

24

CROCODILES EVERYWHERE

It was a late winter evening when we reached Dangamal through the water way from Gupti, the only way those days to approach the place from the Divisional office side. One had to come either from that side or from Chandabali side through the tidal rivers and creeks to reach Bhitarkanika Wildlife Sanctuary. It was low tide when water recedes almost 2 meters. We had to climb from the deck of the 'Boula,' the motor launch at the jetty, through a wooden plank. It was a visit of the Principal Secretary, Forest & Environment, who was thrilled with the journey to the Bhitarkanika National Park. This park set in the east coast of India in Kendrapada district of Odisha covers the estuarine mudflats in the delta of Rivers Brahmani and Baitarani. These tidal mudflats boast of largest mangrove diversity of Indian main land. It also had excellent faunal diversity in the form of mammals, birds, reptilians, amphibians and fish fauna.

As we went up the jetty to walk to our Forest Rest House through a narrow foot path, moon light was filtering through the *Phoenix, Avicinia, Heritiera* branches and also through the planted casuarinas and coconut trees. The cheetals were chomping grasses in the meadow on the left. The crickets were continuously making a sonorous sound. Weather was excellent. The glow worms were flying from branch to branch of *Tamarix*. All this imparted a surreal appearance to the entire area, more so for the city dwellers. A cup of tea was most welcome and it reached us without asking.

As we were settling down with our hot tea cups, a gentleman, dead drunk, trailed by few other men and ladies came rushing to us and started charging me and the Principal Secretary for not giving him and his party the best of suits. Any explanation did not satisfy him. Pradeep Karat, the DFO also tried to pacify him with no effect on him. Despite the effort of his wife and all his entourage he took a long time to cool down and departed to retire for the night.

We learnt that he was a famous physician from Ranchi, whom I do not intend to name. None of us took it very seriously as we knew that he was not under his own control.

We had very good sleep after a hot dinner and seeing the herds of cheetals grazing with their eyes glowing just next to our Rest House.

We decided to leave for inspection next morning after early breakfast. As per plan we started and boarded the boat. As we preceded east, number of crocodiles, very large, large, young ones and juveniles were seen basking on the mud flats flanking mangrove forests on either side. Few small herds of cheetals were seen grazing on wild rice along the banks. The breathing roots of mangrove trees across the mud flats were casting small shadows on the muddy ground due to rising sun. Some trees were supported by stilt roots on all sides. The thick vines were crawling up some trees like pythons, which were very common in the area along with the king cobra, the moist poisonous snake of the Indian sub continent. As the high tide was receding, the tidal water that had inundated the forest floor was flowing down the banks like small springs and making musical sound. Kingfishers in their myriad hues were jumping from branch to branch and flying small distance for better fish catch. We were switching off the engine of our boat intermittently in order not to disturb the wild animals and birds.

Suddenly as we negotiated a bend in the creek we spotted lone private motor launch stationery close to the bank of the river, where a large crocodile with smaller ones used to bask. I saw and recognized the same group led by the physician and sensed some trouble. If there was no trouble there would be no reason for any tourist to go so close to the bank and stop so close to crocodile nesting mud flat.

Disabled bat being rescued.

I suggested to Sri Rath, Principal Secretary that we must go and check up, what they were up to. Since he was not very familiar to the area, he did not think that there could be any trouble. But I insisted and went close to the boat and found the same doctor with his family and friends almost in tears as they did not know what to do as their engine had failed and all efforts to revive it was in vain. It was a highly crocodile infested area. All the occupants, particularly children were very scared as was evident from their looks. Though their boat driver and crew were trying their best to give them courage, they were quite helpless. Of course we knew that no crocodile ever attacked occupants of any boat however small it might be. They were strangers to this part of the country and had no knowledge about the behaviour of the animals here. We docked our boat with theirs and one by one lifted every one into our boat.

Instead of proceeding for the inspection we returned to Dangamal to send the group back to the Forest Rest House. The entire team was very apologetic about what happened the previous night. We told them to forget this as a bad dream and that we have only done our duty. Though we lost lot of time in the operation and delayed our inspection by about two hours, we were quite happy that we could rescue the group, as they were our guests.

On his return to Ranchi our doctor friend wrote a long letter expressing his gratitude and thanking the Forest Department for the courtesy and helpful attitude, which he had never expected in the back ground of what happened the previous night.

A visitor comes to an alien protected area fully controlled by the PA managers with very sparse presence of outsiders. Hence he or she is completely dependent on the park management for safety, security and comfort. It is therefore the duty of the management to see that they return back safely, with lingering sweet memories and proper understanding of the natures elements. Such visits create empathy for all living creatures. While ensuring this it is also our responsibility to see that they do not in any way disturb and deplete the habitat through their action or ignorance. Besides, every PA management should see that they go back with some knowledge on the biological diversity of the area and its role in their sustenance.

———————— ⁺⁺✦✦✦✦⁺⁺ ————————

25

LUNCH IN A GRAVE YARD

It was hot summer months in one of the hottest parts of Odisha in Kalahandi in early seventies. The state had just taken over Kenduleaf working by the Forest Department from the earlier operators mostly from Gujarat and other states. We were yet to know the trick of the trade. As a DFO completely new to kenduleaf working I had to work very hard to learn the nuances of the operation, particularly in summer, when the most important item of work 'collection' is carried out. My team of field staff, except the Head Checkers, Checkers, most *Munsis* and some *Chowkidars*, who were old hands in the trade, were also all new and had to work very hard. Hotter the days with no cloud or rain the happier were kenduleaf staff as any cloud or hail storm locally called '*kara*' at this time would lead to attack by insects called '*kida*' or tear and damage the leaves resulting in reduced output or poor quality of leaves. Our Conservator Sri S.S. Das based in Bolangir was also completely new to the operation and was working very hard to see that we succeed as the earlier operators always told that we shall completely fail. This was indeed a challenge. To add to our owes, we had to pay much higher wages to all workers, as government employers we were supposed to pay fare and legitimate wages unlike the earlier agents who paid fraction of that amount resulting in much higher expenditure. The old agents and their senior staff also further mystified the trade for us as they wanted us to miserably fail so that the government shall be forced to reinstall them. Hence relentless working braving the unbearable summer heat was the only way for us to know the tricks of the trade to surpass the achievement of the old hands.

One fine summer morning our Conservator Sri Das and I left Bhawanipatna at around 5.00 am to see the collection work in M.Rampur and Gudvella areas. Normally I start with water in *'Surahi'*, an earthen pitcher draped around with coir cover and a *'Chhagal'* a cavas bag hung in front of the radiator of the jeep to cool the water through evaporation, a bottle of alkaline mixture to prevent sun-stroke and towels to cover our faces from the hot sun. I used to carry my packed lunch in Tiffin carriers. But since Sri Das was also on inspection, Sri Girija Mohanty the Range Officer of M.Rampur told that he will carry packed lunch, as lunch carried from home at those early hours may get spoilt due to extreme heat by the time we eat. I agreed.

We picked up Sri Mohanty from his headquarters with tiffin carriers containing lunch and additional supply of water. He was himself an excellent cook. Sun was beating down mercilessly.

By around 1.00 pm we were all very hungry. But as we looked around we did not see any shady place to sit down for lunch. It was flat land with kenduleaf bushes with green and red tender leaves everywhere. At a distance we saw a lone Barun tree (*Cretava religiosa*) standing with green foliage. We were happy that at least we could sit down for the lunch there.

Taking lunch in a Grave Yard.

On reaching there as Mohanty opened the tiffin carrier, we settled down on two boulders with water from the 'chhagal', which was very cold due to evaporation process. The food was quite tasty, partly because we were very hungry and on the other due to culinary skills of Mohanty. We saw that Mohanty was not taking anything. I asked him the reason. He said that he fasted on a Monday. I found out later that in his haste not to delay our visit he forgot to carry the second tiffin carrier where he kept additional food for himself.

We had a satisfying lunch and as we looked around we saw that we had settled down to eat in a 'village grave yard' (smasana) where there were signs of burning carcasses everywhere, broken cots '*khatias*', torn clothes and broken pitchers etc.

We knew our mistake but hunger had over powered any logic. We even failed to notice all these signs. We went from *Phadi* to *Phadi* (collection centers) and saw the afternoon collection in Gudvella area and returned to Bhawanipatna late at night. This experience was etched in our memory and Sri Das mentioned it often when we met later.

Of course, through the efforts of everyone who joined in the Kendu leaf wing of the Forest Department in its initial years and really worked very hard see that the trade succeeds, the government earned much more revenue and there was no rethinking on the de nationalization of this trade.

26

EXHIBITION FOR THE PRIME MINISTER

I reached the spacious bungalow of the Divisional Forest Officer, Balliguda at G.Udayagiri up in the Phulbani plateau in the late afternoon. The evening chill had descended on the picturesque rolling hills of the Phubani plateau. Sri C.V.S. Murty and Sri L.K. Patnaik, two senior officers were sitting quietly and sipping heir tea. Seeing me reaching in my green rickety old jeep, they looked happy and asked me to join them. When I asked them about the progress of the exhibition stall of Forest Department at Burbinaju irrigation project site, their reply was depressing, 'nothing!'. I joined them for a quick cup of tea, which I needed most after a tiring journey up the hill and proceeded with them to the site of the exhibition to be inaugurated by Smt. Indira Gandhi, the Prime Minister of India on the next day morning. The little remote place was abuzz with flurry of activities. Most stalls were nearing completion but the stall allotted to us was without even a cloth cover. Bare corrugated sheets used as wall of the stall were staring at us. The villagers and work force who were going round the stalls were commenting that the Forest Department is still sleeping and saying, "This is perhaps the only stall which will be adversely commented upon".

I was then the DFO Afforestation operating from Berhampur and had overlapping jurisdiction of the Phulbani district also. We immediately bought draping clothes sold within the complex and covered the vacant walls of the stall space. There was no dearth of manpower, as there were forest field staffs everywhere. I took an excellent artist Ramakanta with me, who had graduated from an art college and was quite innovative and fast. We sat down and gave him an idea of the theme. He made pencil sketches of the details of the stall interior based on our theme. After doing some amendments, I proceeded to procure two sloth bear cubs which were rescued by a villager in Tikabali. I knew that live wild animals shall certainly be very interesting exhibit. There was flurry of activities in our stall while most others had gone to sleep. When I returned with the cubs by around 10.00 pm the stall had made considerable progress. We made small amendments and asked them to rest only after the stall was complete in all respect.

We returned to G.Udayagiri past mid-night, had a quick light dinner and went to bed to get up early so that we can reach the exhibition site by 7.00 am to see if any last minute amendments or additions required. It was a chilly night.

Winter early morning chill of this hill town was difficult to bear. Fog covered all valleys and visibility was rather poor. We put in our best available formal dresses as we were to receive no less than the country's Prime Minister, Mrs Indira Gandhi and proceeded after a very early breakfast.

Ramakanta and other forest staff had gone to sleep after giving finishing touches. We had a closer look at the exhibits. Some rectifications were required. This was done. The bear cubs were placed close to the entrance. The theme of 'need for protecting hill slopes with forest' was eloquently depicted, clearly showing the prosperity and beauty of a fully clothed hill alongside a deforested and degraded hill slope with its impoverishment. This theme was chosen as the forests of this vast plateau was subjected to wanton destruction though shifting cultivation locally known as *podu* and the P.M. would have seen lot of such barren hills during his chopper ride to reach here.

The stall area was thoroughly cleaned up as lots of debris were strewn around the stall due to late night working and waited for the inauguration, keeping the curtains dropped for maintaining the surprise element till the opening.

Prime Minister's Chopper landed few hundred meters from the site right on dot at the appointed time and after a short ceremony of laying foundation stone of the irrigation project, came to visit the exhibition. She breezed past most stalls stopping for a few seconds where she found anything interesting.

But, it surprised everyone present there to see that she came in to our stall and patted one bear cub I was holding and asked few questions on different wild animals of the area. She spent almost 5 minutes in our stall. Everyone who was commenting on our empty stall on the previous night was awe-struck to see all that has been done in course of the night.

To surprise of everybody the culmination came when our stall was declared as the best stall in the exhibition. People of all departments came rushing to us to congratulate and press people gathered to photograph the stall and ask questions. The little bear cubs were staring in bewilderment from their perches as all attention was focused on them. The staff who had worked hard throughout the previous night and particularly Ramakanta was jubilant as their effort paid rich dividend of attracting the Prime Minister.

Unfortunately Ramakanta is no more in this world as he had a premature death when he was working as an art teacher in a reputed school. In deed there is no limit to possibilities if one sincerely goes about doing ones work.

———— ·✦✦✦✦· ————

27

STUDENTS GREEN A BALD HILL

It was a festive evening in Gopalpur on sea. The Paknati Model High School, perched on a bald lateritic hill was abuzz with activity. The school was decorated with mango leaves and paper banners, the usual way of decorating an institution for any festive occasion. Students and teachers were waiting to receive their guests with bouquets. Number of white Ambassador Cars and few government jeeps arrived in quick succession. Guests alighted from them and went straight in to the school premises. Dignitary after dignitary kept delivering speeches in a language they were fluent with: Oriya, English, Bengali, Hindi, Sanskrit and Telugu to the gathering of teachers, students and some guardians. The occasion was 'Vana Mahotsava' week. The Revenue Divisional Commissioner, District Judge, Vice Chancellor, Conservator of Forests, Collector, DIG of Police; all topmost functionaries of the area and many others were there for this celebration of the ceremonial tree planting week celebrated throughout the country in the first week of July every year. I had taken advantage of this celebration to kick start clothing the fifteen acre bald hill on which the school was built.

I had started this venture as a challenge as this hill devoid of bereft any vegetation other than *Jatropha* shrubs on rock crevices, stood right on the entrance of the beach town frequented by many tourists from within the country and abroad. This was also a favoured beach resort for the British civil servants before India's independence. My staff, particularly the Range Officer, Sri Brahmananda Nayak was very hesitant as digging each pit was quite time consuming and costly and it was impossible to meet this cost out of the existing plantation norms of the Forest Department. To add to that, I asked him to make oversigned pits in order to provide more good soil to the seedlings planted on such a refractory site. This also meant additional cost of carrying good soil and buying manures.

But, I had other ideas. As I saw that there was good demand for seedlings by the people of the locality who wanted seedlings to plant in their compounds, farm bunds and temple premises, I asked for raising a nursery just below the hillock with seedlings far excess in number then needed for the planting. We priced seedlings at 25 paise each. And I calculated that the revenue earned by selling surplus seedlings will far exceed the cost involved in raising the plantation and its maintenance, as the Headmaster assured that the entire hill will be planted up by students and staff and they shall provide watch and ward besides their tending. This support was to considerably reduce our budgeted planting cost.

After the speech session was over everyone went to the planting site. As the guests were doing the ceremonial planting, the entire school kids spread all over the site and started planting with the guidance from the forest staff and their teachers. They even consolidated the soil and watered every seedling. By next day all seedlings were planted up. By the next year Vana Mahotsava, the seedlings had grown up to a considerable height and had made the hill lush green.

School children planting saplings.

The enthusiasm with which the teachers and students were planting them was of great satisfaction, as more than raising a successful plantation, these young kids' awareness that tree planting or protecting forest is a great service to the nation will go a long way to protect our environment. They also planted the seedlings assigned to each of them under supervision of their teachers and looked after them.

The proceeds from the sale of the seedlings from the nursery not only met the planting cost, savings from these proceeds helped us to provide some labour input for soil and moisture conservation and to raise thorny hedges along the road side to prevent browsing by passing goats. Brahmananda who was very skeptical about the plantation was the happiest person to see the result and for praise he received for his efforts.

It was indeed a dream coming true and any senior officer visiting Gopalpur went to see this plantation, which in two years had shielded the school building from the view. It so happened that Sri Natabar Pradhan, our Minister, who was a very work minded person belonging to Boudh came with a group of people of his party to show them this hill and told them tauntingly when this was possible here in such an inhospitable terrain, why not in Boudh?

Many barren hills which struck every one passing through the highway or away from it got clothed. Even few of them are standing today despite the biotic pressures they are subjected to.

The pace with which the forests are being exploited for industrialization, mining and urbanization besides road, railway, canal development, and irrigation projects, it is essential not only to protect whatever forest is left in the country, but also plant up land available for the purpose and take proper care of them in order to save our environment; though, certainly a plantation is no substitute for a natural forest. Such innovative measures shall be very useful for the purpose. The involvement of people, particularly the young ones shall have a snow balling effect towards achieving this goal.

28

GREENING THE HIGHWAYS

Some roads particularly of erstwhile princely states like Patna (Bolangir), Boudh, Keonjhar and parts of Madras Presidency etc struck me as they had beautiful avenue plantations all along their main roads of trees like Neem, Mango, Jamun, Arjun, Ficus etc. Modern day multi row avenue plantations along roads and canal banks in Punjab and Haryana are virtually their only sizeable forest patches. In contrast our modern highways were devoid of any vegetation, though they had wide strips of land on either side, either lying fallow or people doing unauthorized cultivation there.

I thought something had to be done, though there was no such scheme or funds available for taking up such venture. I checked up and found that I shall be saving some funds after achieving my target of plantation for the year1977-'78. As Divisional Forest Officer; Afforestation, Berhampur my main job was to raise plantations in the government land including degraded forests in undivided Ganjam and Plulbani districts. But, would the National Highway authorities allow me to take up such a venture? This thought nagged me as I knew that the land was solely the property of the National Highways authorities. Of course, I had succeeded in taking up a single row planting along a long stretch along state highway from Kalinga to Phulbani in Kandhmal district in 1976.

I went to the Superintending Engineer, National Highways, a very senior engineer. He was very reluctant as he apprehended that there may be public opposition if we started planting where people are cultivating, though illegally. He asked, "Am I competent to allow another department to plant there?" He also felt that the Forest Department might permanently occupy this land given for planting and they may have difficulty to do anything else there when required.

He was assured that nothing of the sort would happen and I agreed to give that in writing. I further told him that as we did not have much money and we could only tackle a small stretch to begin with after his approval of a scheme prepared for the purpose.

The iron should be struck when it is hot. I had taken my stenographer with me when I went to his office and minutes of our discussion were drafted allaying all his fears that would enable us to take up plantation on N.H. land. I agreed to all the conditions suggested by him. A scheme for avenue plantation in the entire state was prepared terming the plantation as "Quasi Commercial Multi Row Avenue Plantation" and sent to all quarters. Of course its approval had never come and perhaps has not come till today. The S.E. was quite happy when he learnt that this would be very first such venture in the state and that would be a feather on his cap and signed the minutes.

It was essential that these plantations should be provided protection as they were linear strips and subject to grazing and illicit removal. It was learnt that some thinning materials were available in Surada Range of Ghumsur South Division. Thinning is an operation conducted in congested forest patches to allow enough space to individual poles to put on girth to make them timber worthy faster and fetch better price. The poles which were removed for making space for other promising ones are called thinning materials. I talked to the DFO, Ghumusar South Division, Sri H.N. Sahu, who agreed to spare them on payment of royalty, which is a reduced cost, much cheaper than the market value. We had some barbed wire in our stock. A Forest Ranger, Sri Suresh Chandra Ratha was a spare hand available and he was willing to take up the collection of thinned material and do the fencing.

Three Nurseries were raised at suitable locations between Berhampur and Chhatrapur and at Huma along NH-5. Considering our fund position and ease of planting we decided to plant in three patches covering nine Kms. We decided to plant in 6 or 7 rows depending on space availability with the first row being the avenue row planted with shade providing long living plants with wider spacing and other rows behind were of fast growing timber or fuel wood species to be harvested and replanted in short rotation.

This was first of such ventures in the state and senior officers who visited this, though were quite happy, were also very apprehensive and told that nobody noticed when plantations failed in the interiors. But if that happens just on the highway, the department shall be subjected to severe criticism. Hence, I got the sign boards fixed at the avenue strips changed as 'experimental avenue plantation'. It was indeed a great success and few remnants of this still exist after more than three decades, despite human and other biotic interference.

This was the very first such effort and next year Cuttack Afforestation Division took it up on small stretches while after two years this became a regular feature along all high ways and major roads under different schemes.

Of course the first single row avenue plantation was raised first by our division in 1976 along Kalinga – Phulbani road. Many trees still stand on the highway. Particularly Mahogany and Spathodia stretches are striking.

But unfortunately with the ever increasing traffic, the old stately avenue trees raised by Marathas, later on by rulers of princely states or by the British are being removed in order to widen the roads. Two-lane, four-lane, six-lane and one do not know where it will stop. But the planning for such widening should include retaining of old trees which provide shade, serves as habitat for birds, reptiles and small mammals, besides other floral diversity. These plantations help recharge ground water and reduce glare and partly naturalizes air pollution caused by vehicular emissions. While they improve aesthetics of any road, they provide much needed shades for those needing to stop on them in case of break down or otherwise. Those linear strips can also to an extent compensate for the loss of natural vegetation due to urbanization, industrialization and mining.

But many avenue plantations raised are lost due to their felling for widening besides illicit removal etc as they are not taken care of by anybody. It is essential that not only we should take up avenue plantation of right design and right species mix but also take care of all avenue plantation raised in the past. Involving the communities of the villages through which the road passes in its protections and incentivizing them may be able to prevent any unauthorized removal.

———————— ++++++ ————————

29

BRAHMANI GHARIALS

as a child I grew up not far away from River Brahmani and among talks on wild animals by elderly grannies were always crocodiles. The talk of these reptiles devouring the entire body of people, particularly women along with their massive traditional silver or brass ornaments like bangles, *khadu, bataphala, notha, pauja* etc and these being recovered from them when killed was common. These talks were mostly imaginary as crocodiles were dreaded animals and problematic children used to be silenced by these dreadful stories. But it was a fact that crocodiles, namely gharials *(Gavialis gangeticus),* muggers and estuarine crocodiles where in good numbers in many coastal rivers in Orissa.

But a survey in 1975 showed that the status of all the three Indian species was rather precarious. Hence a project was launched to save all the 3 Indian Crocodilians with support from the Union Government and Food & Agricultural Organization (FAO) of United Nations. Dr. Bustard a famous herpetologist was brought to Odisha, the only state which had all the 3 species. Only Mahanadi had a very few Gharials left and we had to start the project with eggs brought from Nepal and bringing an adult male from Frankfurt (Germany) on breeding loan to Nandankanan. Of course three centers namely Dangmal for estuarine crocodiles, Ramteertha for muggers and Tikarpada for gharials were established in the same year.

But I vividly remember the day when body of a huge dead gharial, locally called *thantia kumbhira* was brought to my village. The animal was so long that its head and tail were hanging from either and of the bullock cart. Perhaps the year was 1952. The animal was shot by Sri Rajkishore Dhir, a crack shot belonging to *Opara garh* of our village Balarampur, lying on a plateau on the top of a hillock. He was making a show of the reptile in all nearby villages to exhibit his flawless marksmanship. There were huge gatherings to see this animal everywhere the cart went. People, particularly children were touching the body and some daring ones were putting sticks in his hanging snout. Elders were reprimanding them. This went on for 2-3 hours.

This was very clear evidence that Brahmani and even Baitarani, which are interconnected, had gharials. But despite all conservation measures including reintroduction from the captive population, their number is dismal even in Mahanadi. Of course, the other two species have responded well to their conservation initiatives and revived in the wild. There is no question of gharials inhabiting Brahmani again due to pollution load and threat to its water flow as too many industries want to draw water from this river. I have serious doubt, if action is not taken from now, the ecological flow so essential to nurture the mangroves of the Brahmani–Baitarani delta and even agricultural crops of the delta may be threatened due to high saline ingress, resulting due to want of fresh water inflow. We may have to ponder about this and take appropriate step to save these rivers and the aquatic life forms and mangroves dependent on them.

————————————— ⋅⋅⋅⋅⋅⋅ —————————————

30

DRIVING A TRAIN

It was late December, 1964 afternoon. A passenger train with a steam engine was about to leave Balarsah, a station from where timber and bamboo transport to other parts of the country was the main business, in Maharastra for Kazipeth in Andhra Pradesh. Our coach, in which a section of senior class students of the Indian Forest College were travelling on their shortened South India Tour was shunted and attached to that train. The engine was spewing smoke and the furnace which was heating the boiler was being fed with coal relentlessly by the Khalasis. The cabin was full of coal dust and was very hot despite the winter chill.

The train was already late and we were apprehensive that the connecting train that would take us to Madras (now Chennai) would depart from Kazipeth before our train reaches there.

I went to the Driver, who in railway parlance is called Loco Man. He was a middle aged Anglo-Indian gentlemen and very friendly. He was able to effortlessly communicate with us in English or Hindi. I was the 'orderly officer' for the group at that time.

The job of the orderly officer in the Forest College is to take care of the group, its logistics, discipline and work as a bridge between the teaching staff and probationers (trainees). Of course this assignment was rotating one and changed every week.

Hoping against hope I told the Driver that we are going to Chennai and unless our coach can get attached to the connecting train we may have to be stranded at Kazipeth and not only forego the Madras visit, our subsequent program may be seriously dislocated. Considering the delayed running of the train, could we still make up?

He said he would try his best and as a second thought invited me to join him in his cabin in the engine, definitely an unenviable place to be in, considering the heat, noise, dust and smoke. But, I agreed to join him. A very fine talkative gentlemen, who promised to tell me all about train movement and signaling etc.

As I went in to the engine where he showed me all the controls of a locomotive and he said 'this is the bar which acts as an accelerator and you are free to accelerate but we have to honor the signals in all stations." Considering the maximum speed of an old stream engine we were making good progress through the lush green Central Indian forests and made up almost 45 minutes. But, alas! As we were entering Kazipeth we saw the tail light of the connecting express train leaving the station, with the Guard on its rear coach waving green lantern signaling for further unhindered movement of that train, as night had set in. The Driver was very sad and bed good bye with a warm hand shake as I alighted from the engine to join my friends in our coach, which was detached there.

We checked up the time table to find that there is no express train to Madras till late in the afternoon, which meant that, if we are attached to the first train we can only reach next morning, with no time left before taking the next train to Coimbatore on way to Ooty (Now Uthagamandalam). We resigned to our fate and left it to the railways to decide our connections.

They decided to attach our coach to a passenger train, which will take as up to Vizaywada from where the train would take a different direction towards Howrah. Our coach was detached and taken to a siding in the morning. As I went to the Station Superintendent's Office to enquire about our further connection, the Chief Ticket Inspector came to check our tickets and all my friends told him that the tickets are with Patnaik.

He kept on looking for me, and when he located me introduced himself as Martand Rao Patnaik. He was very happy to see me as he had married in Cuttack; though he did not know Oriya and belonged to Andhra Pradesh. He took me to his official quarter and offered South Indian breakfast in his house and introduced to his family and assured me to do his best to make us reach Madras as early as possible.

He talked to the Station Superintendent and pressed him to attach our coach to a non-stop Parcel Express, a goods train mostly carrying perishable items with very few stoppages. But the railway officials understood our predicament, which was not due to our fault and attached our coach to that train. I was worried that we may not be able to have our lunch as it was a non-stop train. Thanks to the railways, they talked to their restaurant in Ongole station, a very small one to keep early lunch ready for us so that we can get down and take quick lunch and return to the coach. The train was instructed to stop there for half an hour and ensure that all of us are aboard before the train departed. The train stopped at that station and we all filed in to the little restaurant that had arranged our lunch of hot South Indian dishes on the floor on green banana leaves, a totally new experience for those from North India. We boarded our coach within the allotted time and train departed after the Guard ensured that all of us were in the coach.

It was to the surprise for everyone that everything thereafter worked as planned and we reached Madras in the afternoon rather unexpectedly for our accompanying teaching staff who had reached earlier and were staying in the retiring room in Madras Central station.

Subsequent journey, which was curtailed to 25 days against normal 45 days, due to shortage of coaches for meeting huge requirement of passenger coaches for the Eucharist Congress being held in Bombay (Mumbai) for the first time was quite eventful.

All my friends who were in the group still remember the journey which had many more surprises too. The nostalgic memories of now defunct steam locomotives, chugging their way across length and breadth if Indian countryside, continues to linger on in our mind.

————— ✦✦✦✦✦ —————

31

INSTANT WAGE HIKE

It was perhaps the World Forestry Day on 21st March 1993 when Sri Biju Patnaik, the legendary Chief Minister of Odisha was invited to Nandankanan. He was to do a ceremonial planting of a Sal sampling near the western gate of the beautiful park. I accompanied him along with other political people and officers to the planting site. He went there is his famous old Willy's Station Wagon, christened as 'Kalinga Rath'.

After the tall leader alighted from his car, he walked down to the planting site and performed a small *'pooja'* and did ceremonial planting of a Sal sapling and it's watering. After that he walked in the opposite direction of his vehicle and then got off the road. I pointed out to him that the vehicle is on the road on the opposite side. He did not pay any heed to me and proceeded to the place where a group of tribal women laborers were standing. The octogenarian then placed his hand on the shoulder of the oldest of them and asked her how much she was being paid. She replied, it was Rs. 11/- per day. He then asked if she is paid Rs.25/- would she be happy. To that she asked who will pay her

Rs.25/- more than double of what she is getting. To that pat came the reply "Everyone will be bound to pay as I am Biju Patnaik telling this". I don't know how much they believed his words but seemed quite happy and were all smiles as such a high dignitary talked to them and even placed his hand on one of them.

Then he returned to his car with me to go to the meeting venue. There he made an announcement to the surprise of everyone present that "Considering the plight of people working as laborers, I have decided that the minimum wages shall he enhanced to Rs.25/- from tomorrow".

He returned to Bhubaneswar and the notification was issued the next day enhancing the wages.

This surprised everyone as the decision was not preceded by any prior discussion, cabinet meeting or paraphernalia usually associated with such decisions. He did mention in the meeting that he was moved by the plight of an old lady whom he met few days back during his tour to Khariar area, a chronically drought affected area of the state. This is unconventional but true and this dare devil leader, who happened to be a very daring pilot and a successful industrialist before joining politics and happened to rescue Indonesian leaders from their own country to be decorated later with *'Bhumi putra'* the highest civilian honor of that country. Even his body was draped with the Indonesia's national flag along with our national flag; a unique honor for this daring statesman.

————— ✦✦✦✦✦ —————

32

Journey to Hukitola in Kasyap

Our largest Motor launch Kashyap of the Mangrove Wildlife Division was in the sea and taking a beating from the huge waves. Its cabin was high above the water level in the level of the lower deck where I was seated with DFO Sri Sanjeev Chadha and other senior staff. It so happened that the surf generated by high waves even entered the cabin and went across the cabin drenching us all. Panic had gripped everyone. Different senior people were giving different instructions to the launch driver. I had to tell everyone not to speak nor panic and leave everything to his judgment.

It was maiden journey of Kashyap into the sea though this boat was designed as a sea going vessel, everyone was quite apprehensive of its sea worthiness. During one of my tours to see the new nesting island, I decided to take Kashyap to Hukitola from the divisional headquarters at Rajnagar. Hukitola was an island in Bay of Bengal, with a very old and majestic building owned by the salt board of the British days. To meet the fresh water requirement of the inmates in an island surrounded by hyper-saline sea water, this building had its own rain water harvesting and storage arrangement, with a large water tank underneath the massive structure. To approach this one was to travel through river Hansua and then through the coastal waters of the bay.

As we crossed Hansua river mouth, we saw the unusual sight of large number of fishing trawlers entering the river as if in a procession. They were from different bases as seen from their markings. We were surprised. I asked our launch crew to stop one of them and ask the reason. The trawler stopped and told that sea is going to be rough and that is why they want to take shelter in the calm waters of the river. Of course there was no visible sign of any such storm. We were already in the sea before we decided to return back.

The waves pounded on the left (eastern) side of the launch which was heading north to Hukitola. Everyone was panicky as, ML Kashyap, though a huge boat appeared to be unsafe for any sea journey, as the experienced boatmen felt that it cannot stand the beating from the coastal waves. Most of them started praying for a safe journey and return. Even some suggested returning back in to the river, which we had left some distance behind. But we felt that the sea before the river mouth would be more turbulent and we may have to face rough sea for a longer distance if we return. Instead the course ahead was safer bait. The launch driver agreed with me. The boat was rising almost two meters to ride the trough of the waves and then dropping down to the crest and the sound was deafening. We could not hear each other and were completely at the mercy of the waves and strong wind, which appeared from nowhere. At one point we even thought that the wooden planks of which Kashyap was made may not hold together much longer and the launch may break. We were all wet. Fortunately the driver of Kashyap who was quite experienced held his nerves and followed the course to the Chatka, a sheltered area of calm waters, flanked by Hukitola group of islands on the east and the mainland on the west. We were all drenched with hyper saline water by the time our boat entered calm waters of 'Chatka'. We heaved a sigh of relief and after inspection of Hukitola, with its 150 year old massive British day bungalow. The view of other nearby islands with loss green mangroves and the calm waters of Chatka, and mainland beyond was indeed breath taking. It was completely different sea almost as calm as still waters on our way back. Of course, the launch driver had to be careful to avoid any contact with a wrecked ship that hit ground perhaps a century back when she mistakenly steered in to these shallow waters.

The return journey to Rajnagar was pleasant though uneventful. The trawlers which were going in to the river for shelter when were on our out bound journey were returning back in to the sea to resume their fishing activities again. Every one narrated his mental state at the time when the boat was being tossed about by waves and gusty wind. Of course, Kashyap passed the test. But we decided not use it in the sea and keep its movement confined to river and deeper creek system in the mangrove ecosystem of Bhitarkanika.

We all learnt a lesson that panic is worse than the catastrophe itself and a panicky person can commit fatal mistakes. At that point the thought of *nolias* or fishermen going in to deep sea in their little catamarans crossed our mind. How did they dare to go miles in to the rough sea without any safety equipments or navigational aids with only loin cloths on their body? Seer guts help them to take up the journey every day for a living. The staff that accompanied in that journey remembers the event even today.

33

DUMKA ELEPHANTS

I was in Ranchi on a request by the Chief Wildlife Warden, Jharkhand, Sri Biswas. Perhaps the year was 2004, and I had retired as Chief wildlife Warden, Odisha 3years before. A herd of elephants was cause of concern for them, as this herd of 16 pachyderms were wondering around entire Dumka region from one forest patch to another and causing havoc by trampling people, breaking houses and raiding crops. The forest patches had sparse vegetation cover and most of them were plantations in isolated patches. There was no elephant in this area for more than a century, nor there was any connectivity in the form of contiguous forest with any other known elephant habitat. It was presumed that they had come either from Dalma near Jamshedpur or from North Bengal 10 years back and have almost become resident here. Of course, such migrations are not uncommon in India these days as elephant herds have moved to places far away from their original habitat. The examples are migration to Chhatisgarh, Maharashtra and even Goa and Chittoor district of Andhra Pradesh to mention a few. Habitat degradation, encroachment, illicit removal of forest produce, disturbance due to blasting for mining, movement of earth movers, lighting and fragmentation due to road, rail or canal has forced them to abandon their old habitat and move to newer tracts. This also resulted in severe human elephant conflict resulting in damage to crops and other properties and death or injury to people, who had not experienced such depredation in their life. The resultant retaliation caused death or injury to the pachyderms.

Sri Biswas and I took an overnight train from Ranchi and reached Dumka. We had a discussion with all local officers and studied map of the area along with movement pattern of the elephants. It was learnt that they are moving everywhere in a single herd along with young ones. We visited some villages recently predated upon. We also saw a country liquor shop called *'Bhatti'*, where 4 persons were killed by them due to trampling and wall collapse few days back.

We kept on enquiring about recent movement of the herd as people knew well about them due to very sparse vegetation in the forest or plantation patches in the area.

At about 4.30 pm Sri Sinha the DFO told me that the herd is close to that village inside a teak plantation about a kilometer from the road on which we were travelling. He suggested that we should go to the site. I told them that this was the time for the herd to move for foraging after their rest in that forest patch during the hotter part of the day and so we should be careful while approaching them. Sinha of course told that they do not move so early here.

We trusted him presuming that he had more intimate knowledge about their movement pattern and proceeded towards the forest patch up the hill. I was ahead of the whole group which included Sri Biswas, DFO and other forest staff and some villagers. We reached a narrow village road flanking the forest patch. As we went up the clearing, suddenly the elephant herd sensing trouble flapped their ears and trumpeted. They were about 15 meters away from us. I stopped and shouted at the top of my voice to our group *'hillo mat'* and *'ruk jao'* in order to stop them wherever they were. As I knew that if we run back they will charge, which may result in casualties as they can run as fast as horses for short distances. The elephants also registered my loud command and froze where they were and all of us also stopped. It was good 10 minutes of standoff.

Then we decided to slowly walk back while few of us continued to watch them still standing quietly. They were obviously concerned about their young calves. We were fortunate that they did not charge us as that could have become fatal for few of us including me who was not in best of physical condition to out run any elephant, particularly in rough hilly terrain.

We returned back to Dumka and met Mr. Babulal Marandi, the Member of Parliament who was earlier Union Minister of State for Environment & Forests and discussed the problem in greater details.

Finally we settled down with forest maps and revenue maps of the area and talked to field staff about their movement routes in different seasons, the area most vulnerable and worked out a plan of action, which included short term, medium term and long term actions so that the damages can be minimized. They may involve sensitizing the people, improving the elephant habitat in the forest patches of the division, tracking the animals, informing people well in advance, advising people to store grains in secure places like *pucca* bins or secure community godowns and not to store country liquor in their houses besides charting their movement routes etc. As there was no connectivity with any other known elephant habitat any effort to drive them away to any other area would have been counterproductive and may involve much more damage to life and property.

As the elephants have settled down in the area and are living here for a decade, it was felt necessary and prudent to train people to live with them in harmony with altered cropping pattern, life style and least possible conflict. For this to be effective, I advised the forest officials to be vigilant and provide compassionate grants to people suffering loss of crop or property or to the families of those killed without any loss of time. Unattended complaints could make them hostile towards the elephants.

———————— ✦✦✦✦✦ ————————

34

CELEBRATING NEW YEAR

Makut is a sleepy little place in Kerala on the western side of the Western Ghats, which happened to be a regular camping site for the trainees of Indian Forest College, Dehradun to study the famous Nilambur teak of Kerala, the finest quality of teak wood of the country and its management. Our batch was no exception. We were camping there for a couple days before New Year to study the lush green rain forests of the Western Ghats. Our camp was about a 200 meters from the Forest Rest House located on an elevated ground that housed our Instructors.

It was New Year of 1965 and we got up to a fine morning, to the chirping of birds on the surrounding trees and wished each other for the new year and after morning routine up to breakfast left for the FRH. As we reached there we found that Sri Kaushik, the Director, Forest Education, who looks after forestry education of the country, was standing there along with our instructors in full field fatigue. He was known to be very strict with the trainees and was a quite hard task master. Obviously he had reached the previous night.

We greeted him on the occasion of the New Year. Pat came his greeting "I Wish Happy New Year to you all. But, have you cared to know where we are?" He pointed to the India map hung to a black board fixed for the purpose and showed us Kerala, Western Ghats and Makut. Then he started describing the characteristics of the forests of the region.

That was just an introduction to be followed by lectures after lectures including by former Working Plan Officer of the area with only brief breaks for tea, lunch and dinner till it was 11.00 pm. We were all fagged out and talked among us that perhaps the entire year will be like this as it is said that 'Morning shows the day'.

Next day there was a field trip to the Tropical Rain Forest of Western *Ghats*, running almost parallel to the southern coast of India with its stately tall trees of most species we had not encountered before. As the road was rough and narrow we had to travel in tractor trailers into the forest. We were all in *Khakhis* with *'sola topis'*, hats made of pith called *'sola'* to withstand any impact and to protect from summer heat, used those days by serving forest and police staff in most states. These hats are obsolete now. The foot wear was ankle leather boots with iron studs for grip. Woolen putties were fastened above the boots with the bottom of trousers tucked in. This prevented leaches, ticks and mosquitoes, which were common features in forests those days and protected from thorns and mud besides giving support. Of course leaches and ticks are common features in many forest areas even now, more particularly in the North East India.

We stopped at a point beyond which even tractors could not move and proceeded on foot in a formation like the army columns move. After moving few kilometers we suddenly found a lone person clad in *lungi* and half shirt in a clearing perhaps collecting some forest produce. Seeing us advancing towards him, he was scared and folded his *lungi* up and ran for his life to stop and look back at us at intervals. As he saw us still proceeding, he again did the same thing and ran for few hundred meters, as apparently he was very much scared to see so many uniformed people running towards him. After the 3rd stretch of run he perhaps found a foot path to escape from the wider path and vanished. It was indeed a sight to see and all of us who have seen this still remember the scene and laugh to our hearts' content.

Tropical rain forests are location specific forests confined to the western part of the Western *Ghats* and North – East India. These forests when cleared do not regenerate and often taken over bay alien invasive species (weeds) and hence needs utmost care as they support very rich biodiversity unique to these regions. In contrast to the eastern part of these hills which has scanty rainfall and support dry deciduous forests, the western side receives five times more rain. This ecosystem also supports unique fauna, many of which are endemic to the region. Unfortunately our tour to this unique forest type was so short that we could hardly understand its unique ecology. But later on in early eighties in order to save a pristine patch of rain forests of Western *ghats*, known as 'Silent valley' from being sacrificed for an irrigation project in

Kerala the union government had to enact an act called 'Forest (Conservation) Act, 1980'. This is a land mark legislation that has prevented wanton sacrifice of many forests in the country on flimsy pretexts.

———————— ·✦✦✦✦✦· ————————

35

BLACK BUCKS OF CHANDRABHAGA

The morning sun had just come out of the Bay of Bengal South of Chandrabhaga beach, as we were walking down the beach with the Chief Minister, Sri J.B. Patnaik accompanied by Mrs. Patnaik, Collector and Superintendent of Police, Puri, the Divisional Forest Officer, Wildlife, Sri Sidheswar Mohanty and C.M's skeletal security personnel. This was a stroll after a highly satisfying early morning wildlife trip. The C.M. had changed subject and lamented about India's poor show in Seoul Olympics. The S.P. Sri Sahu was giving his opinion as to how the sports personnel should be groomed for such events. We were all engrossed in the discussion in very pleasant ozone filled invigorating environment of the beach along the coast of the Bay of Bengal, despite a very short sleep in the previous night.

It all began the previous evening when I suddenly received a phone call from the C.M's office that the C.M. would like to see the black bucks in Konark – Balukhand W.L. Sanctuary. I myself had never seen one there, though I had seen their signs. I told the Private Secretary, that perhaps it will be better if we first decide on the exact site to be seen before C.M's visit. To my surprise, he told that the C.M. has already left and expect me to be in Konark tonight. It was not a part of my administrative jurisdiction. Hence, I went to Sri Sidheswar Mohanty, D.F.O., who was looking after the sanctuary. As I reached his residence, I found him down with a bout of asthma. Though I decided to go alone, he took some medication and got into the vehicle. We reached Konark P.W.D., Inspection Bungalow to find that the C.M. was yet to reach. We waited till 11.00 p.m. when he reached with his entourage after attending some work on the way after a tiring journey.

He was very happy to see us, and asked when we should start. I told that it will be ideal if we leave by 4 am. On further questioning I replied that they are not too numerous and I have myself not seen any. Hence, the best chance is very early in the morning when they will be in a meadow. He agreed and despite his age and late night sleep, he was ready by 4 in the morning. All of us were ready and vehicles were in position. We started for an opening where about 200 meters away from the marine drive I had during my earlier visit had seen the signs of black bucks.

We went to the spot about a kilometer south of Chandrabhaga and stopped. I requested that only few of us should go in the first batch to be followed by a larger second batch without any talking or making any noise.

The sun was yet to rise and breeze was blowing through the *Casuarina* trees was making a sound of its own which masked the little noise we produced while trading on the *Casuarina* needles lying on the sandy surface. All of us maintained pin drop silence and further slowed down before approaching the sandy meadow where an artificial water hole was made particularly for *cheetals*. We decided not to go out into the open meadow and watch from the cover of casuarinas not to scare them away. Our strategy paid off. We saw 9 black bucks, 3 stags and 6 does chomping tender grasses on the shores of water hole. It was indeed a sight to behold. The second group of the people had already reached and also had a good view of the herd. Everybody was very pleased about the conservation efforts.

The coastal sandy stretches of Puri and Ganjam district perhaps hold hardly any black buck, but they are being replaced by *cheetals* very fast due to want of open meadows as closely spaced *Casuarina* plantations raised as a part of coastal shelter belt as protection against coastal cyclone has virtually left no blanks or grassy patches favoured by black bucks, who are fine feeders and stay in open meadows, requiring very little water for their sustenance. Some efforts are being made to open up few meadows and reintroduce them there. Hope, it will yield positive result and receive support from the local community.

This visit and few more satisfying ones to other P.A.s convinced the C.M. that given a helping hand nature will take care of itself to support rich bio-diversity.

36

ODIA PITHA AND LOW TIDE

It was nearing mid-night in the tidal river of Pathasala in the mangrove forests of Bhitarkanika. We were close to the mouth of the river near Ekakulanasi. The ML Kashyap, the Forest Department launch lay anchored. Boula the other large launch of the Forest Department was slowly swaying in the river water, not too far from the Bay of Bengal. Cool breeze was blowing from the south. The engine sound of the little mechanized boat, known as *bhutbhuti* locally had stopped and there was eerie silence other than that produced by ripples of river water hitting the stationary swaying launch. The silhouette of coastal casuarinas on the east and of mangoves in the south and west was reflecting on the river water, lighted by faint moon light. The Chief Wildlife Warden Sri L.K. Patnaik and I were waiting for the small boat to return from the beach dropping the Union Environment and Forest Secretary and Additional Secretary on the beach to witness the mass nesting of Olive ridley marine turtles. As the boat was too small to take all of us in one trip and the water was too shallow for Kashyap to cruise in, we had to wait for the next trip.

It was for the first time that the Secretary to Government of India was visiting the division to see the spectacle of mass nesting of marine turtles of which Odisha is proud off. Sri Rajamani a very tall person with keen interest in wildlife conservation along with Dr. Ranjit Singh, Additional Secretary, who is a noted wildlifer of the country, were vising the sanctuary. We all reached Rajnagar, headquarters of the division in the evening and went straight to a small guest house of the revenue department. Sri Bitanath Nayak, a very keen wildlifer and innovative person was heading the division. To our surprise instead of the normal evening snacks Bita babu had arranged the Odia delicacies called *pitha* (country made cakes) of different types like *chhunchi patra, chakuli pitha, kakara, bara* and *arisha pitha.* The guests were so pleased to see the unique preparation that we all had our stomach full of these delicacies along with evening tea. After this was over our guests wanted immediately to go for seeing the nesting but Sri Nayak told them as per the advice of our launch driver to start around 11 pm so that we should reach the river mouth at the time of high tide, when there would be sufficient depth of water to allow passage of a small boat up to the site, a narrow strip of sand bank between river and sea, where nesting was taking place for about a3 to 4days. It was largest nesting ground of the species in the world and the phenomenon was called *'aribada'*, a word adopted from Spanish. Sri Rajamani was perhaps not prepared for this delay, as he knew that this phenomenon lasts for a few days and already three days of nesting was over. He asked for advice of Dr. Singh. He dismissed the advice of the launch driver and said that we must immediately proceed and nothing shall go wrong.

As he was a very experienced wildlifer and field-man the secretary tended to agree with him and we proceeded to Gupti and boarded Kashyap, the largest of boats of the Forest Department there. It was an uneventful journey except that we passed on lot of information in bits while on conversation with them, till we reached river mouth from where it was not possible for Kashyap to negotiate the waters as it was too shallow. A small boat with a seating capacity of barely four persons was waiting for us. Since the guests from Delhi were very keen to see the nesting we decided to go in two trips. Sri Rajamani, Dr. Singh and Bita babu went in the first trip while Sri Patnaik and myself stayed on in Kashyap waiting for the boat to return back to pick us up. Hardly the boat had left us and sailed for five minutes from us it stopped. The water was too shallow even for this little boat to navigate. It stuck in the muddy floor of the creek. We could hear them talking and they could hear us but there was no way for them to come back to us or for us to approach them. This went on for good 3-4 hours till the high tide started reaching and there was just enough water for the little boat to float. They were quite hungry, despite sumptuous *pitha* meal in the evening, as all food stuffs were left behind in our launch. Instead of proceeding further they returned back to Kashyap very hungry tiered and drowsy. It was around 2 am in the morning. Everybody praised Bita babu that the *pitha* he gave us held us in good stead till that time. We decided to return back to Dangamal, the Forest Rest House again a few hours sailing upstream abandoning all hopes of watching the nesting as this does not usually take place during the day. Of course the ride was smooth and fast as the rising high tide pushed us from behind. We reached Dangamal by dawn, when the morning mist was hanging over the water surface obstructing clear view, birds had started chirping and hopping from branch to branch to pick up insects and cheetals on mud flats had started to go into the bushes for cover. We did our morning chores before sitting for a sumptuous breakfast. We had a hearty laughter when we remembered the previous night's experience. Everyone was full of praise for Bita babu for the imaginative *pitha* service, though sorry for missing the spectacle of *'arivada'*. Perhaps we would have done well had we given some *pitha* in the small boat which carried the Secretary's team. We could also imagine the plight of a very tall person like Sri Rajamani spending about four hours in the cramped space of a very small boat.

The life in this eco-system is always like this. It is governed by the tidal position which changes every day with the lunar position. The high tides occur twice every day and recede twice to low tide. The mangrove vegetation supported by such ecology has developed adaptations to meet such a scenario through viviparous germination, breathing roots, stilt roots, and modified foliage. The salinity level also varies at different points and different times of the day and night. Hence the vegetation is completely different in different patches and the dependent fauna also vary to a great extent as they have to adjust to these harsh conditions. It boasts of a rich faunal diversity comprising of estuarine crocodile, water monitor lizard, king cobra, python, few species of dolphins, fishing cats, large numbers of migratory as well as resident avifauna besides fishes etc.I have always admired my staff who work untiringly in such conditions day and night to protect this small mangrove sanctuary, now also a National Park and a Ramsar Site surrounded by thickly populated tract of coastal Odisha, oblivious of their own safety and well being. I salute the highly innovative wildlife officer, Bita babu, who is no more in this word with us; for his passion, hard work and dedication to wildlife conservation with utter disregard to his own comforts and safety. May his soul rest in peace in his heavenly abode.

———————— ⁺⁺✦✦✦⁺⁺ ————————

37

CONVERTED BEAST

It was a quiet late winter evening in the little Revenue Bunglow in Mohangiri on the fringe of Kalahandi district. It was an old Victorian structure, on the fringe of a dense forest, constructed by the Kings of Kalahandi state in this village bordering the then Patna state. The shadows of chairs, tea table, tea pots and people sitting around formed due to the light emitted from the old kerosene lantern were giving an eerie feeling. It was a relaxed atmosphere after a long day's work involving stock taking of the preparedness for the approaching working season for kendu leaf operation. Kendu leaf is the leaf of a plant that is used in South Asian countries as wrapper for country made cigarette that is in good demand and an excellent source of income for local people. A wood fire was lit for keeping us warm. Film songs of Radio Ceylone, a popular radio channel, were playing from the portable transistor radio. Few of our contractual field staff who had accompanied me for the field visit was sitting round the fire to warm themselves. I usually got fascinated by the local folk lore and this relaxed atmosphere was very ideal for storytelling.

I was in charge of the newly created Bhawanipatna Kenduleaf Division as my first divisional charge after my promotion. We had recruited many contractual staff like Supervisors, Head Checkers, Checkers, Munsis and Chowkidars, who were earlier engaged by the Kenduleaf Agents as the operation was in private hands before my joining. Most Agents were *Guajaratis* i.e. people from Gujrat state in the western parts of India and they almost monopolized the trade before its nationalization in 1972. This time was also excellent for interacting with such people who gave away lot of information about the method of working by previous agents. This was quite informative and helped me plan my work strategy for the year ahead.

In our congregation was one Sri Basant Patnaik an experienced Head Checker. It appeared that his fore fathers had migrated from the coastal tracts of the state and settled in Madanpur – Rampur area and Basant was working with the Agent in that area for quite a few decades. He was eager to tell some Shikar stories. I encouraged him and all those present heard him in rapt attention.

He went on in a very low voice narrating one of his experiences. "Almost 20 years back, when the population was much thinner and forest all around was much denser with small pockets of agricultural land, number of wild animals like Wild boars, Cheetals (spotted deer), Sambars and Barking deer used to descend to the agriculture fields surrounded by small habitations for foraging on standing paddy crop. Most people used to set up *machans* or raised platforms on wooden stilts and maintain vigil after early dinner to scare the animals away by fire crackers, beating of tin cans and shouting etc.

Our group of young people used to take advantage of this and go out for *shikar*. It was one such night when we were on our hunting spree. As we positioned ourselves on a *Machan*, suddenly we heard the slurp slurp sound of a lone wild boar entering into a field and chomping the standing rice paddy plants. There was faint moon light and I focused the spot light on the animal and another companion pressed the trigger of a pre-loaded muzzle loader gun. The shot hit its target and the pig fall to the ground. They all went down and took the animal for feasting on it on the next day.

But in the evening a wailing woman approached all of us and said that we had killed and eaten her husband. We were all surprised and asked her, how can that happen. What she narrated was difficult to believe."

She narrated while sobbing, "My husband had enmity with Kundru for long time. This year he had an excellent crop. As it was ripening, he wanted to teach him a lesson. He did a *pooja* (a particular type of ritual) in the evening and turned himself into a wild boar and went for foraging into his field, leaving a bowl of sanctified turmeric water with me. He instructed me to sprinkle this water on him after he returned so that he will again become man.

But, I waited and waited for the entire night and he did not return till morning.

I have made a thorough search, but he is nowhere to be seen. Later I learnt that you have killed the boar that was destroying his field and having a feast."

223

Basant added "It was impossible to believe her story as it does not stand to any logic. But her husband never returned."

It was a story that sounded like an imaginary story, far from any reasoning; though Basant asserted that this happened and people in that area still practice such witchcraft in different forms to cure diseases, to ward off evil spirits and even for causing harms to their enemies. Though it was very difficult for me to believe the story, Basant became very remorseful after narrating this story. It is said that they were even becoming tigers, leopards and other animals as was necessary for which they learnt the process from their senior practitioners of the tricks very painstakingly as in these remote areas, education had not reached, doctors were very rare, roads were absent and civil administration was virtually absent. I have heard similar stories from many other remote areas but never with so much detail.

----- ‥✦✦✦✦‥ -----

38

SAVED FROM THE GALLOWS

It was early in the morning on a December morning in 1995, when I was woken up by persistent ringing of my telephone. I got up to hear the voice of my Principal Chief Conservator of Forests Sri N.C. Patnaik on the other end. "Saroj, your elephant which was coming on a truck has created problem on the outskirts of Bhubaneswar and trying to break the side walls of the truck. The truck driver and the people passing on the road were very scared. He had been informed this by Khandagiri Police Station. He asked me to do something very fast as there was panic among the locals and as the day progresses there was likely to be more problem. I was in fact very worried about the transport of a tusker, who was captured near Bolangir and was being transported in a large trailer truck fixed with a cage of stout angle iron bars. Though I was concerned about him, I was confident that he cannot break the stout cage. Of course my doubt was cleared soon after when the Forester Sri Nair telephoned from Aiginia and conveyed that as Prema the captive cow elephant was passing, she heard the sound of stone crusher close the highway and wanted to jump out of the truck that was carrying her. She was very docile compared to Basanti the other elephant who was also coming in another truck accompanying the newly caught bull. They had both been sent to help bring the captured tusk-less bull from Bolangir. I was worried and advised them to take the truck to an elevated place, preferably a soil dump for using the same as a ramp and unload Prema from the truck. That was done and she was controlled, before I reached the place.

The bull elephant that was captured was the lone elephant without tusk and was moving in the entire undivided Bolangir district for several years and raiding ripened paddy, vegetable gardens, ground nut and other crop farms and when confronted, attacked people injuring them or causing death. His massive built also frightened people. This was particularly more alarming as the entire district did not have wild elephants for several decades. Though people in that part of the state revered elephants, they were very concerned about their own safety. He was very regularly targeting a beautifully grown farm of an advocate on the outskirts of the district town, which is rather a very dry and water scarce area. There was persistent demand from the public to declare him dangerous to human life and property, under the Wildlife (Protection) Act, 1972 and eliminate him. Of course the Forest Department always hesitated to issue such an order without making very sure about the animal's behavior. Public pressure was so insurmountable that after getting all details of his antecedents the orders were issued. But, no one could execute the elimination order within the time period allowed in the permit. He roamed free and still created panic and couple of human deaths took place due to fall of walls or trampling.

We discussed and the Chief Wildlife Warden decided to capture him by chemical immobilization. Sri B.N. Nayak, wildlife trained officer and a very devoted and daring wildlife manager tried his best to tranquilize him. But all his efforts failed. And at one point of time he was saved just because he fell into a compost pit to escape from the track followed by the elephant.

The bull continued to be elusive for another year and kept on creating havoc in the district and neighboring tracts. When demand to eliminate him grew even stronger, I as Director, Nandankanan Zoological Park had to depute the Range Officer Sri Kamal Lochan Purohit to accompany Dr. Lala A.K. Singh for the immobilization operation. Through persistent painstaking efforts with the active support of the then Divisional Forest Officer Sri Sisir Acharya and his field staff, they could finally immobilize him. The place of capture was Kharsel Reserved Forest not far from Bolangir town. According to the name of the forest block, a low dsensity tropical Sal forest, we decided to name him Kharsel. He was tied to stout Sal trees with chains and sisal ropes. I immediately dispatched two cow elephants Prema and Basanti, with their *mahouts* and assistants to give him company and control him. The site where he was tied became a place of pilgrimage and people came with coconuts, sugar cane, bananas and paddy for him. Even small *paan* shops, tea stalls and eateries sprang up there to cater to the thousands of daily visitors. A local daring person 'Nila' was engaged to assist in his up keep. He picked up the art of controlling and caring elephants very fast from our *mahauts* and continued to look after Kharsel till I knew last for more than two decades. Bolangir district heaved a sigh of relief as he was finally captured. Our Veterinarians from the zoo and local vets provided him health care and he was provided food, water and water was sprinkled on his body from time to time all through the day. But the constant dragging and pulling the chain to escape injured his feet, which usually happen in such cases of capture. This was reported by the press and few even went to the court in public interest litigation (P.I.L.) as they termed this as cruelty to an animal. But, I knew that we were doing our best. But still felt that even if there is negligence I perhaps would be able to know in three or four days as the animal was 300 kms away and the mobile phone had not yet made its advent in India by then. I decided to bring him closer. Nandankanan was out of question as to get such a powerful untrained animal into a place visited by large number of people every day with nearly 2000 wild animals housed there might be risky in case of any escape attempt by him. I decided on Godibadi the entrance of Chandaka Sanctuary, which had been named Elephant Reserve by the State Government. We had requisite staff presence there. It was not too far from Nandankanan for veterinary care to be made available fast. We constructed a shed and made a ramp to facilitate unloading of Kharsel.

Kharshel after capture. Photographed by K. L. Purohit

The task of transporting such a huge, powerful untrained *makhna*, a tusk-less bull over 300 kms of busy road was definitely daunting. We did not know how to do it. We thought of several options and finally thought that it has got to be a cage made of stout iron members built on a trailer truck, so that there will be no chance of escape or attack to any one on the way.

A design was worked out and with a lot of difficulty a trailer truck owner willing to transport the bull was found and the welding work got underway at Barang under supervision of Sri Purohit. By the time several animal right groups have been writing to the state government for taking action regarding improper treatment of Kharsel.

I had already told the DFO to reply to the Public Interest Litigations in the court that we may authorize any one to care for the elephant better than what we are doing through the court. That had silenced the litigants.

I advised the DFO to dig a ramp close to where the elephant was tied so that the animal can be easily pushed into the inbuilt cage.

I proceeded to Bolangir and the trailer truck followed. But it had difficulty in negotiating crowded places like Khurdha and Nayagarh where overhead power lines crossed over the roads. The power had to be shut down before the truck passed creating lot of resentment among the public. We knew that that cannot be done on our return journey with the elephant, as it was necessary to bring him fast, as he had to be partly sedated to avoid unduly exciting him. Hence my first work was to take exact height measurement of the elephant and reduce the height of the cage to the extent feasible. This was a herculean task, as cutting and refixing such a heavy structure without a crane in a remote place like Bolangir was almost impossible. But we had to improvise and made a tripod structure to hold the cage, while we cut about 50 cms from the bottom and re-weld the cage in place firmly. This took almost a day's hard work on a way side welding workshop.

We knew it will be a whole night job and set up tents close to the place of capture and had our food there. By around 11.00 pm the trailer truck was rolled into the sloping ground and its platform was kept at the same level as the ground.

We stuffed the platform of the truck with eatables favored by elephant like banana plants, sugar cane, *ficus* branches, jaggery and paddy rolled in the paddy straw close to the cabin so that to reach them he has to step inside the cage.

A briefing session followed. I instructed everyone to operate is total darkness and in complete silence. Purohit, Nair, our driver Rout and two other staff went under the trailer with the instruction that they will tighten the chain tied to the fore leg of Kharsel, as he advances towards the food stuff, some of which were kept just outside the truck and at the entry to the platform. After he finishes all that he would be tempted to venture into the cage without suspicion. We figured out that after putting two fore legs on the platform he would not be able to retrace, as his large head will hit the sides of the cage. At that point of time force should be applied through two captive elephants and *mahauts* so that he would have no alternative other than going in. Then those waiting under the truck would tighten the chain completely and the planks would be placed behind him to prevent his return.

This operation started immediately after every one had dinner and all other than the team including me who were assigned the job, went to sleep. It was complete darkness, even the Kerosene lamps were kept inside the tents. My eyes had got used to the darkness and I could see his activities faintly and direct the team below. He was tempted by the food stuff and as he was inching towards it the chain got tightened as I was guiding to the team trough sign language or whisper. The operation needed lot of patience, as those under the truck had to sit in a very inconvenient cramped position tormented by mosquitoes, while maintaining silence. The captive elephants with their *mahauts* were ready for the final push. It was almost at 3 am when he put his fore legs on the platform. I knew that he could not retrace from there if he is pushed. I directed both Prema and Basanti to charge. They came from behind with their *mahauts* on their back and pushed the animal and Nila also prodded him with the stick and command which he had learnt from the senior *mahauts*. Seeing no alternative, Kharsel entered in to the truck in just five minutes. We immediately put three steel rails behind to secure him firmly and waited for our doctor to sedate him with a mild dose of *xylazene*. It was dangerous to go inside. So the vet had to enter the truck through the back opening with care flanked by trained mahouts. Despite that Kharsel tried to press him to the side planks of the truck with hind parts of his body as he was pushing the injection in to his rump. By 4.00 am, before the day break the operation was over. When D.F.O. Sri Mohan got up hearing the noise and jubilant exclamation of staff, he was surprised to see the *makhna* inside the cage.

We decided that the vehicle should cross Bolangir town before day break as there may be large crowds gathering in the streets and it might become difficult to pass through its streets, if people get up. The team was advised to stop at a rice meal far beyond the town limits on the way where the staff accompanying Kharsel can complete their daily chores and breakfast in complete isolation and if necessary give him another shot of sedative and cold water spray for keeping him calm throughout the journey. Things went according to plan and I left the entourage at the rice meal, but saw people waiting in large numbers on way side to see the elephant, who had become quite infamous in the area for his destructive activities.

After sending Prema and Basanti from where Prema created problem on her truck to Nandankanan, I proceeded to

Godibadi where the trailer of Kharsel had already arrived and positioned against the ramp. With very slight effort he went out of the cage and straight to the shed where he was to be tied like an obedient child. Perhaps, his exposure of last few days, his caging and transportation over three hundred kilometers had given him enough indication that man is the master to whom he has to submit. News of Kharsel's arrival spread like wild fire and almost entire media was there to cover every detail of his story. Pictures and story of the *makhna* appeared in all national and local print and electronic media and hailed the state forest department for its effort to save the huge pachyderm from the threshold of elimination.

A training session for Kharsel started at Godibadi. A master trainer from Assam Sri Bijayananda Choudhury alias Dudul Choudhury imparted training to him through his trainers. He has written in a newspaper column that "The greatest challenge in my life was to train an elephant like Kharsel". Nila continued with him and also got trained in caring and managing elephant.

Kharshel after training. Photographed by K. L. Purohit

After few months we decided to put him in use in Debrigarh Wildlife Sanctuary near Hirakud Reservoir for its protection work. A ramp was prepared near Godibadi and a full bodied truck was positioned there. We prodded him to board the truck. Once on the truck he felt insecure and dashed the cabin and side walls and stepped back jumping the back board with his hind leg and we were so scared at that time that if he puts his leg in the space between platform and the ramp, we will have no way to extricate his huge legs. Besides we did not know as to what would happen to the large crowd gathering all around. The owner of the truck came to tears, as his truck was bettered. We were very scared and deferred our move for the time being.

Nila continued to take care of him in Godibadi till it was decided to take him to Debrigarh on foot as he appeared to be too scared to board a truck, perhaps remembering his transportation from Bolangir. Once in Debrigarh he was the monarch of all he surveyed, as there was no elephant in the sanctuary and bamboo, his preferred food and grasses were plentiful. The huge Hirakud reservoir, on whose bank he was kept was an excellent water body for his bath or even for swimming. Elephants, despite their massive body are excellent swimmers. Even they do swim in sea water while crossing creeks to go from one island to another in Andamans.

Debrigarh was prone to encroachment by fisherman who made huts along the banks of the reservoir. There was also timber and bamboo theft as the staff strength of the Hirakud Wildlife Division was low. Kharsel's presence became a boon for the department as all these encroachers and smugglers were scared of him. I went on a tour to the sanctuary. I was passing through the forest road. Suddenly in the fading light of evening Kharsel appeared from the opening in the bamboo thicket. It was a massive and scaring form. I could realize why forest offenders were so scared of his presence.

We wondered how this lone elephant was roaming in Bolangir district for so many years, though there was no wild elephant reported from there for several decades. People who saw him earlier could recollect his story. He was brought by a *mahaut* perhaps from Bihar or Eastern Uttar Pradesh to the district. Usually many such elephants come to Odisha and move in villages and cities. People due to their reverence for elephants as *vahana* (vehicle) of Goddess Lakshmi give them food, paddy, rice and money. This collection provides enough for the *mahauts* living and sending to the actual owner the rent for taking the elephant for the purpose. In this case as he was camping near a village for a few days, the *mahaut* developed close relationship with a local girl and in the process got arrested by the police. The elephant perhaps named 'Shankar' was left without any keeper. He broke his chain and wondered free. He was not used to forest life and often raided agricultural crop fields thereby coming in conflict with people and killed several people when obstructed. As he was a captive elephant he had lost fear of people. As the years passed he became wild and his old identity was lost.

Hundreds of such elephants are reared by people in north India just for the purpose of begging. Some are kept in Rajasthan and Delhi for marriage, religious or political processions. Most of them live in appalling conditions, constantly chained and made to walk on hot asphalt surfaces. Many of them are made to walk even when they are sick. Their illness often goes unattended. South Indian temples also do keep large number of tuskers for their processions. Their conditions are somewhat better, though they have no chance of procreation. This results in a loss of wild population of males, which already suffers a skewed sex ratio. In Assam and North East where many privately owned captive elephants were earlier engaged in logging and many other works are just without work now and their owners do not have means to look after them.

These problems must be suitably dealt with so that this beautiful largest land mammal which is our heritage should live with dignity and cared for in their wild habitats.

———————— ‹‹♦♦♦♦›› ————————

39

THE CHIEF SECRETARY CAME CALLING

I was in a thick plantation raised in a valley near Khallikote and giving instructions to my staff to clear a passage through this for jeeps to pass along that inspection path. I had reached from Phulbani the previous night after getting a call from Sri D.P. Bagchi, the Collector of Ganjam.

As DFO, Afforestation, Berhampur Division, I was looking after both Ganjam as well as Phulbani districts. I was on tour to Phulbani to attend a district meeting there. Sri Bagchi had called up my residence and when learnt that I was on tour to Phulbani, sent an urgent message to DFO, Phulbani to call me to his telephone so that I can talk to him. I came to the residence of the DFO and booked an urgent call to Chhatrapur to Sri Bagchi as there was no trunk dialing those days and one had to wait endlessly for a booked call to mature. An urgent call was somewhat better. He told me that Sri Dave, the Chief Secretary is coming on a sustained tour to the district starting two days after. Sustained tours those days used to be compulsory for very senior officers and spanned over a week and covered most important aspects of administration of the district. Sri Bagchi wanted me to arrange inspection of plantations of the district for a day. As some excellent plantations were raised over last several years in the district, on the waste lands and barren hills of the district, I told him that the Chief Secretary can be kept engaged for the entire week if he wants to see the plantations. He was very happy about my offer and told that, he would start his tour with our program.

I had to rush back to reach that night as I had only one day left. I sent message to my Range Officer and reached the morning before the visit. The inspection paths were covered with weeds and rain cuts, making it impossible for vehicular movement. We had just one day to make it negotiable by Mahindra Jeep an usual mode of movement in the forest areas and rough terrain those days. More than ten kilometers of path was cleared to take us across different ages of plantations raised over the years. It was so thick that the sunlight was not falling on the ground in most cases. Within that day a good information sheet with map showing the plantations taken up in the district, highlighting the areas to be visited was prepared and made presentable. Computers or even electronic type machines had not reached our markets till then making things really difficult. The district officials were very apprehensive as this was the first program to be reviewed in the district. But when Sri Dave reached it was found that he was limping due to a fall in bathroom that morning and Mrs. Dave accompanied him for support. After initial introduction, Mrs. & Mr. Dave boarded my jeep with Sri Bagchi that I drove.

I had to be very careful to see that he does not have to walk due to his ankle injury and his injury does not aggravate due to traversing very rough road. Of course, it would have been wrong to call it a road.

As we drove through the mud track, flanked by thick plantations on sides, two years, three years, four years old and so on stopping at few places to gauge the height, girth and success rate. It gave look of a naturally grown forest. The branches of planted trees were spreading over on to the road for getting sun light and were giving a tunnel like appearance and feeling. Few red jungle fowls ran across our path and partridges gave their call *Kiu-Kiku.......Kiu-Kiku........*reverberating throughout the valley. A cheetal stag also jumped across our path giving us a feeling of a high forest. Success was nearly 100%.

Sri Dave was so pleased that he started asking me names of different species and their uses. By the end of the day we had covered all the plantations of the valley and Sri Dave told that they had not ever heard of these success stories sitting there in the secretariat in Bhubaneswar and these should be published and field staff rewarded for such good work. He thanked Sri Bagchi and me profusely for making it possible for him to see these plantations raised over barren waste land that had transformed the entire tract.

Thirty five years have passed since that visit, Sri Bagchi still mentions about that wherever we meet.

Not only plantations, giving helping hand in the form of protection from biotic interference can create excellent forests in hardly any time. The bright example of Chandaka which was once covered with dense *Eupatrium* weeds can open eyes of every one. It is now full of kanta bamboo and good tree cover despite biotic interference still continuing to some extent, due to its proximity to the densely populated state capital city of Bhubaneshwar. Just protection has transformed a waste land in to a vibrant wildlife habitat. In recent months even a tiger and her cub have been reported to have migrated there from distant Satkosia Wildlife Sanctuary. It was actually a lone tiger that has become captive in nearby Nandankanan Zoological Park.

In order to improve our moisture regime and to control pollution from various sources, we may have to take some such steps of protecting degraded natural forests and do inter planting of indigenous plants or take up planting *de novo*. Unlike in the past perhaps money is no more a constraint, if there is will. Involving the local community in the form of Joint Forest management shall certainly improve the protection scenario.

40

CHEQUES FOR PHADIS

It was an afternoon in the month of March in 1972 when I met Sri S.Jee, the then Additional C.C.F. and head of newly taken over Kendu leaf operation of the state by the Forest Department at Bhawanipatna P.W.D. Inspection Bungalow. Sri Jee asked me "Saroj, you have issued cheques for the *phadis* to the ex-agents?" When I replied in the affirmative, he was very unhappy and told me how I dared to issue cheques for such huge amount of more than one lakh rupees. Truly, this was a huge amount those days. I thought, why he should question me when that was the instruction from the government. The rates at which I bought them were far lower that that was fixed.

We had just taken over the trade of Kendu leaf, the leaf that is used to wrap bidis or country made cigarettes. Earlier this was done by the state through agents and purchasers, most of whom were Gujratis or people of other states. While the department was entrusted with the work of collection and processing of these leaves, which had excellent market in the entire south Asian region, the Forest Corporation did its marketing through auction.

Neither did we have any experience or knowledge about kendu leaf production and its processing nor did we have any place to store them. All such temporary storage godowns for raw leaves called 'phadis' belonged to the previous agents. Since we had no field staff, we had to re-employ some experienced field functionaries called Head Checkers, Checkers, Munshis etc who were employed by agents prior to the government takeover of the trade. We neither knew their antecedents nor knew how much they shall be loyal to us. To store the leaves when they were purchased and dried, we needed to construct new 'phadis' as we had none. Five hundred and odd in my division was a huge lot and was the largest number in any division in the state. Sensing this trouble the state government through an order instructed all of us to buy old phadis from agents, if they agree to a certain maximum sum for cubit length for different classes.

As I was Assistant Conservator of Forests in that division a year back I knew most of the agents. I talked to them and made them agree to accept 25% less than the price fixed, as I told them if they don't accept this the phadis shall be ransacked by people for timber and other materials and they shall not be able to get anything. Most of the land where they were erected did not belong to them too. They saw reason in my argument and agreed. Without losing time I issued cheques as they could otherwise change their mind and we would have to procure forest material afresh and start constructing them within one and half months or so. That would mean loss of time for the meager inexperienced field staff besides unnecessary loss of forest materials.

But my Additional PCCF appeared to have sensed fowl play as no other division had been able to purchase any 'phadi'. I was surprised and very sad. My Conservator Sri S.S.Das, a very upright and decent officer who was also new to this trade had also no clue. After, I returned from Sri Jee's bungalow I telephoned to the Agents and asked them if they have presented the cheques for encashing. They told me in the negative and that they are not encasing them as they expect better price from the government. They had submitted protest letter regarding the low price when they received the cheques. I was relieved and requested the Agents to return me the cheques. They returned them in the morning and I went with them to meet Sri Jee. He was having tea with Sri Das. I wished them and told that I had received back the cheques, which I would be cancelling.

Sri Jee and Sri Das looked at me and suddenly realized the situation as they knew that the government may have to spend five times the amount to construct new phadis and the effort that would go into it shall affect the quality and quantity of production. They saw that I was hurt. Sri Jee was a very strict officer, known to be very hierarchy conscious. But, he looked at Sri Das and before Sri Das spoke anything said "Saroj, I am extremely sorry that you are hurt. I have discussed with the conservator last night and come to the conclusion that perhaps you are the only one who has been able to make the agents agree to accept such a low price. Please return the cheques to them and I withdraw what I have told". Of course, it meant re-negotiating with the agents to accept the cheques back without enhancement.

Kendu leaf operation involved payment of cost of kendu leaf every day for which small coins were essential as each plucker had to be paid very small amounts and they were very poor people, who depended upon these small sums for their bare sustainance. But there was acute shortage of the same in the banks in the state. The old agents' people said that we cannot manage the trade without these small coins. I made a specific request to the State Bank of India, who told me that they can be procured from Reserve Bank at Nagpur provided they are requested and police escort arranged through 3 states of Maharashtra, Madhya Pradesh (Now Chhattisgarh) and Odisha. It was a difficult task. But, my request to RBI through the SBI and to the police helped me to procure freshly minted small coins in gunny bags. As there was demand for this by many other departments and construction contractors, I had to clearly tell the SBI to meet my requirement first. The coins were so new that the pluckers sometimes doubted their genuineness and said that they are counterfeit ones made in a place called 'Tarabha' in neighboring Bolangir district suspected to be clandestinely producing counterfeit currency and coins.

Another incident occurred during that period at Kegan, one of my range headquarters. The central godown there was quite large and was holding huge stock of good quality processed kendu leaves. For some unknown reason it suddenly caught fire and burnt everything in it, costing several lakh of rupees. The massage of loss reached the state headquarters when the state legislative assembly was in session. The Range Officer's relationship with the local Officer-in-charge of the police station was far from cordial. He threatened him to report that this was a planned incident to cover up the non-existent bags. I had to meet the Superintendent of Police, Sri Senapati and apprised him of the matter. He ordered re-enquiry through another senior officer after transferring the former incumbent and found no truth in what the OIC had reported. In the mean time the Minister ordered drastic action against all staff from DFO downwards to report this to the assembly. All my staff was scared. Of course I had insured all my central godowns and their contents. Based on the police report the insurance company paid the entire cost of leaves lost in the fire. Everyone was greatly relieved.

Those days whenever ministers came to district towns they usually held meetings with officers and members of public together so that the grievances of people could be redressed fast. In one such visit of our minister number of complaints were made against many departments. The last was about kendu leaf. A young man of minister's party stood up and said that the organization is showing loss due to hail storm or insects and misappropriating money given for collection. The minister asked for my reply. I was surprised and immediately asked for the names of phadis in which such things have taken place as without specifics it will not be possible to enquire. He promptly rattled out names of eight phadis, all of which were not far away from Bhawanipatna. To that I replied that these are some of our best collection centers and if the minister desires we could visit them straightway. I told him that we indeed have few phadis where such things have been reported and our internal enquiry was in progress. In any operation involving more than five hundred centers few cases could always happen and action shall be taken against erring staff. The minister was visibly upset and told the young leader not to come up with complaint in future unless there is truth and closed the meeting abruptly.

Sri Jee's trust in me was doubled and he and Sri Das hardly even questioned any of my decisions during rest of my entire tenure. Despite very tiring schedule starting from four in the morning with *chuda* and *dahi*, water in canvas bags call *'Chhagal'* hung in the front of radiator of my jeep to keep it cool, Alkasol to provide alkalinity to prevent urinary problem and sun-stroke in hot summer days and returning late at night, the results were rewarding. The old agents also envied our operation, though we paid the wages stipulated by the government, which was often more than three times what they used to pay. Thanks to hard toil of every one, the changeover was superb. The leaf that decided fate of many governments in the state stopped doing that any more.

When there is a will there is a way. All those who started this operation and made it a success deserve commendation as it was an uncharted territory strewn with rough boulders and gorges to be negotiated.

⋅⋅✦✦✦✦✦⋅⋅

41

A NIGHT IN JENABIL

It was shivering cold that December evening in 1967 and we were heating ourselves in the wood fire lit under the timber rest house, supported by stout Sal wood pillars to make it safe from elephant herds which frequent the place, surrounded by local tribal people of Jenabil a village in Similipal. They had brought some cooking utensils for us and a chicken for our dinner.

I was Assistant Conservator of Forests in Rairangpur of Mayurbhanj district and Sri Ghanashyam Nayak, an elderly officer, who was my counterpart in charge of National Park based in Jashipur. We had made a joint tour program into Similipal. He had a petrol powered jeep, while I had none. Our program was for three days for an in-depth study of the problems faced by this large contiguous forest, which was designated as National Park by the state government, much before the Wildlife (Protection) Act, 1972 was enacted. A DFO was kept in charge of this National Park starting from late fifties. Later on it was kept in charge of an ACF till it was notified as a Tiger Reserve under the Project Tiger in 1973. As we were to traverse long distance through the hilly terrain of Similipal, we knew that we shall need refueling midway during the tour. As forests of Similipal had excellent timber, it was being worked through contractors by making selection coupes. System selection was a silvicultural system in which only selected trees of certain girth (circumference) and above were marked for working without leaving permanent blanks in the forest canopy. Coupe meant a unit of timber working area earmarked for working during a particular year. We had requested one of the timber contractors, whose trucks operated around the area to deliver a jerry can full of petrol at Jenabil.

We inspected the working of selection camps in Chahala area, discussed field problems at Nawana and took a rather unusual route to get better opportunity to see wild animals. Evening was setting in when animals usually become active, we saw a family of Sambars and then suddenly a group of four ratels (honey badgers) appeared in front of our jeep. I had not seen this animal earlier. These black small secretive animals with white backs ran on the road in front of us. Sometimes they turned back, looked at us and behaved like gesticulating, baring their jaws. This went on for about 2 to 3 kilometers till they were tired. They all turned right and dispersed into thick vegetation through an animal track. After that we went to the vast expanses of Bachhurichara meadows with eerie looking frost bitten forest tract, with stunted trees of unusual forms. This happens as winter frosts burns most trees due to its severity in this valley when frost descends. Though it was biting cold, our stay in a small forest department hut was enjoyable. Next day we went around some of the important areas and saw timber working before reaching Jenabil timber rest house by around 4.30 pm. It was a stately 'Chang' type two storied rest house entirely made of stout logs, planks and corrugated iron sheets as roofing. The ground floor was meant for parking vehicles etc. and was a protection against elephants. It stood on the edge of a large tract of cultivated fields. This was a revenue village. Such a structure called 'Chang' type in North East India was made to prevent any attack by elephants. We had to get ready to spend the chilly night on the open wooden verandah of the rest house, as the Chowkidar had left for weekly market at Jashipur about 40 kms away and was not expected to return till next afternoon as we could not inform him in advance about our program as there was no communication network. Life was hard here in this forest for the forest staff as they had to trek long distances to get their rations or to meet their families. We could not also go anywhere as petrol left in our jeep was quite low. We had some spices and potatoes in our ration boxes, which was invariably carried while touring those days. We washed and mashed the spices and stuffed the bird with it and smeared some mustard oil and roasted it in the fire. We roasted the potatoes too. We also had some bread. We had a dinner of the stuff and after washing our hands and feet with hot water made in the pot provided by the villagers and opened our bed holdals containing beddings and quilts, which accompanied all field officers those days while on tour and lied fully covered to escape from the severe cold and mosquitoes.

Next morning was sunny and pleasant. But we had no toilet to use or anything for the breakfast. We did our morning work like bath in the nearby hill stream and had a breakfast of some bread, mixture and cucumber lying in our ration boxes and walked down to the forest nearly five kilometers away. We knew that no lunch shall be available till late in the afternoon nor we shall have fuel for our vehicle till then. We had a good visit to the forest studying the animal signs, finding natural salt licks etc. We did see few sambars, barking deer and elephants besides the pugmarks of tiger, many red jungle fowls and pea-fowl.

Fully exhausted and hungry we returned to the rest house late in the afternoon to welcome cups of tea, hot *parathas* made of pure ghee and vegetable curry. The *chowkidar* was scared and very apologetic as our experience had been narrated to him by our driver. The food tasted like never before. We also saw two jerry cans full of petrol lying near our jeep. We stayed for the night in the comfortable suits and continued the inspection next day and returned after an excellent tour.

Of course, after Jenabil became a part of the 'core area' after formation of 'Similipal Tiger Reserve' in 1973 along with eight others of the country, this beautiful Forest Rest House was stopped being used for this purpose as visit of people, other than those who looked after the reserve, to the core area was banned. Now that village has been completely relocated outside Similipal, there is a vast meadow surrounding the structure. This shall definitely become an excellent wildlife habitat. Expeditious action need be taken to relocate other villages so that the entire core area remains free from habitation, thereby allowing the wildlife there to reproduce freely and get abundant food and cover for their sustenance. This very large forest patch while saving its rich bio-diversity will immensely contribute to improve water regime of the entire tract while moderating the climate and helping minimize the pollution level.

————————— ✦✦✦✦✦✦ —————————

42

Spike Barrier

It was indeed a very disturbing sight when we approached a beautiful Forest Rest House at Chahala on a plateau in Similipal Forest of Mayurbhanj with Sri Sivaram Mohapatra the then DFO of Karanjia Division in 1968. I was a very young forester who had barely completed 3years of service after training in forestry from the Indian Forest College, Dehradun. The doors and windows were broken and all furniture badly damaged by elephants. The Chowkidar informed that, when a small elephant calf entered the bungalow in search of rice through the door opening and could not find his way out of it, he trumpeted for help. His calls alerted the herd grazing nearby. They broke the doors and windows in order to extricate the calf and in the process badly damaged the furniture, furnishing and utensils of the FRH. The sight was pathetic. We did not know how to prevent the approach of elephant herds to the building cluster. We thought of trenches, but knew that they have to be regularly maintained or else the elephants can easily cross them by breaking it and filling it with earth. We thought of a more permanent solution. Sri Mohapatra assured of funds we needed for the purpose as we needed to use this FRH frequently for inspections and marking operations.

Many alternatives were thought of. I thought if we can develop a strip all around the complex, which the elephant cannot cross it will serve the purpose. We may have to provide only one approach for officers to enter the complex though specially designed gate, through which elephants cannot enter. I also went through the literature to know the minimum width of the strip, so that the elephants cannot clear by jumping, dimensions of elephant foot pad etc. Of course the available literatures were rather few.

I thought if we can put a nine feet wide impregnable strip, it cannot be crossed by elephants, Will stout spikes serve the purpose? What should be the spacing of spikes? How should they be anchored to the ground? I thought that if we place them in 6" x 6" spacing in a staggered manner, no elephant can cross. This can be done with a R.C.C. base. A removable trolley can be used as an entry gate to the complex.

I showed the drawings to Sri Mohapatra. He gave a green signal and allowed me to proceed to Jamshedpur, a famous steel city, then in Bihar state, to procure the materials required.

I proceeded and bought nine inch long nails and got them galvanized in a workshop in order to prevent their rusting and to give them longer life, as they were supposed to be exposed to rain and dew. Procured welded mesh rolls of 10' width for use as reinforcement of the structure.

The strip was difficult to make due to acute shortage of water in that area. But finally the welded mesh was spread on the demarcated strip and the nails placed at six inch spacing as the elephants cannot place their feet within this intervening space. It was completed in a short time and no elephant could actually cross it to go near the FRH or all other structures. A removable trolley gate was made for crossing this strip in order to approach the FRH complex.

This worked admirably well. Similipal became a Tiger Reserve in 1973 and the complex was converted to accommodate tourists. This strip of spikes continued to guard Chahala till early nineties until the steel rusted and there were some accidents involving tourists who inadvertently traded on the spikes and injured themselves.

It so happened, I was taught about this barrier as "Chahala barrier" in 1983 in the International Workshop on Elephants held in Jaldapara in West Bengal.

When I visited Chahala in November 2012, I wanted to see if there is any remnant of the same still left. The staff took me to the backside of the FRH, and showed few stretches still intact and covered with debris.

Every situation in the wilderness may require entirely different approach and one has to handle the same. Of course, there is always apprehension and grave risk of failure too.

43

THE DROP GATE

Chandka Forest on the outskirts of the State Capital Bhubaneswar, its floor covered entirely by weeds in 1983 still had a good elephant population of 57 individuals. These pachyderms were creating havoc all around the forest as they used to stray even in to the city. The state government decided to form an 'elephant reserve' and through suitable barrier confine the animals within the reserve. Hence it was decided to erect elephant proof trenches wherever soil permitted and sausage barriers, meaning wide and high wall of loose boulders, where the ground was rocky. The work started in 1983.

But one problem kept on nagging me. What types of barriers are to be provided when the approach roads shall cross the trench or where there is no possibility of any of the barriers as the natural streams would cross the boundary? Many alternatives were thought of which either allowed passage to the elephants or hindered movement of official vehicles.

I thought that a stout steel drop gate over the trench can serve the purpose. This could be opened for passage of vehicles across the trench and thereafter raised to prevent elephant escape. But I did not know how to do it. Two young men used to do some construction work in Nandankanan led by one Sri Asish Reid of Cuttack. He knew how to develop mechanical devices as he did design few squeeze cages, cages for keeping a large cats like tigers and lions restrained for treatment, which worked well. After prolonged discussion and preparation of alternate drawings we arrived at a design of a gate to be operated through pulley. While dropped, 10 tons of load could pass over it and when raised it would work as an impregnable barrier for elephants. Each adult elephant weighed around three tons. It was designed for manual operation. First such device was installed at Godibadi, the main entry into the reserve and worked admirably well.

The next to be tackled was the water passage. While free flow of water was not to be hindered the elephant would have to be prevented from escape and kept confined in the reserve. A structure was innovated. This involved fixing stout angle iron posts to a concrete foundation across the water passage, at an interval of 75 cum each. Pointed spikes were welded to the inner surface of these posts and all posts were tied with barbed wires forming a mesh. This successfully prevented movement of any elephant across while there was no hindrance to the flow of rain water.

None of them were standard structures and had to be innovated to meet the situation that wanted such innovation.

These barriers protected the sanctuary from biotic interference to a great extent and as a result the degraded vegetation got a chance to establish. Now large tract of this sanctuary is full of bamboo (Kanta) and other trees of coppice origin threw up new shoots to establish as forest. Even a patch of Sal trees, believed to have been wiped away forever, threw up luxuriant shoots. Just a helping hand has helped nature to take care of itself and a natural forest can never be replaced by a planted forest.

44

THE FRENCH CONNECTION

Belghar is a little non descript tribal village tucked in a corner of hilly Phulbani district, close to the border of Kalahandi district of Odisha. It had a nice two roomed wooden forest rest house in a clearing surrounded by luxuriant Sal forests. Being located high above the sea level almost at about 800m and being surrounded by lush green forests, the place was much cooler than its surrounding areas. Surrounded by green vegetation and punctuated by occasional clearings made for shifting cultivation, the view from the rest house was breath taking. I was there about 150 kms from divisional headquarters of G. Udayagiri to work out the changes or improvements to be made to the rest house to host the Ambassador of France and his family who came on a *Shikar* trip. It was before the time of enactment of Wildlife (Protection) act, 1972 and hunting with permit was allowed in India. An ambassador enjoyed very high status as far as protocol was concerned and a dignified state guest. Hence the Director, Protocol of the state, a senior IAS Officer was to conduct his visit. I had a good look at the furniture, furnishings, crockery and cutleries besides the condition of the interiors. I took decision on the changes that can be done in a week's time to make the rest house presentable. This was a place, close to no major city of the state. The nearest were Raipur in Madhya Pradesh (now in Chhatisgarh) and Visakhapatnam in Andhra Pradesh. We had to work fast. I decided to make one suit the pink suit and the other the green suit. Put the carpenters and painters to work and proceeded to Raipur to procure required furnishings and crockery befitting to the rest house. I preferred Raipur as its market was fed by Bombay (now Mumbai), a very stylish city. Every small requirement had to be listed and procured as there was no possibility of getting any if anything is missed. My D.F.O. Sri S. Bose gave me free hand, so that I do not wait for his approval. Those days in 1971, telecommunication was rather very poor. Neither there were mobile phones nor trunk dialing. As a result most communications were through special messengers. The rest house got ready in all respects a day before the VVIP and his entourage was to reach.

Our wait ended when the Ambassador arrived with his wife and daughter after a long and arduous road journey from Bhubaneswar, the state capital. He was an old gentleman beyond his sixties with a long diplomatic carrier. Our DFO and forest staff, police and district administration was in attendance, besides the state protocol led by Sri Hota, Director. We had to stay in the barracks and tents as the entire rest house was occupied by our guests. They were ecstatic to see the place and the timber house. My apprehension of whether they would like the place so painstakingly done up by me was put to rest. One suit had everything including walls, furnishing and crockery of light pink, while the other had everything of pastel green. Local tribes presented a dance around the fire place, before we proceeded for the *shikar*. Of course, the Forest Department used to issue permit for hunting on payment of certain fees under the Orissa Shooting Rules prior to enactment of the W.L. (P) Act, 1972. Unfortunately for the guests the visit did not yield any result. But they enjoyed seeing the vegetation on either side of their meandering route and the sheer pleasure of driving though them at dead of the night. Before the Ambassador concluded his tour, I was summoned to return to Kalinga for attending to the Governor's program there and I had to drive back in our old jeep at night.

We and our families met the Ambassadors' family in Phulbani Circuit House for evening tea on his invitation halfway through his return journey. They were very pleased with the visit and presented little French mementoes to each lady as a gesture of appreciation of our hospitality.

+ + + + + + +

45

I WAS DIRECTED TO TURN LEFT

It was a mid night in 1979 when we were standing in the sanctum sanctorum of a temple and offering 108 champak flowers to the chant of *Shlokas* of the *Pujak*(servitor); an unexpected event.

I was posted as D.F.O. of Ghumsur South Forest Division with its headquarters in Bhanjanagar, a sub-divisional town. My family eagerly waited for a meeting in Berhampur, the nearest city when children had their schools closed, for an outing. We used to visit Gopalpur sea beach, a beach popular with British officers prior to our independence, meet our friends there, shop and if possible see a movie before returning at night. It was an 80 kms journey and took us about two hours.

It was one such day when I attended the official meeting and we saw a popular movie before we left Berhampur little late. Almost 35 kms away from Berhampur, there was a hill range, a part of the Eastern Ghats on our left, while Rushikulya River flowed on the right. I was driving my little Premier Padmini, a version of Fiat. A village road emerged from the highway and went straight into a cove in the hill. The entire area was lighted with myriads of fluorescent lights as a *'yagna'* was going on there. I had a plan to visit the *yagna* later with family during the day time.

But, as I approached the bifurcation point, I felt as if someone is directing my hand to turn the steering to the left. I, without any intension to do so, found myself on the village road. My wife Manju asked me, why I have turned left at that hour of the night? We were to take our dinner after returning to Bhanjanagar. She was worried that children shall be hungry as it was quite late at night. I told them that we shall come later, but there is no harm in seeing the site of *yagna* and accompanying *yatra* there in Karanjei as we shall return immediately as there will be hardly anyone at that hour as it was almost mid-night.

We reached the site of the fair, a forested area in no time. On our arrival, an old lady, who was packing up her shop under a tree at the end of day's business asked us as to why have we came at that hour of the night, as everyone including the priest has gone away. But I told her that I just wanted to see the site. As we got down from our car and went close to the temple, someone from the sanctum sanctorum of the temple called me and asked me to offer 108 *Swarna Champa* (golden coloured champak flowers) as he had the flowers. I told him that I am not the person he was looking for, but he called me repeatedly and finally said that the flowers are meant for me, whoever I might be. Manju also goaded me to wash my feet and go inside. I went inside and did the *pooja* and offering in a very somber atmosphere.

After the *pooja* I requested the priest to tell me why he called me in as I was to come later and I had no prior programme to come there that evening. I had never requested for the flowers.

To that his reply was that the Trustee of the temple had asked him to arrange 180 *Swarna Champa* flowers and he would come to make the offering. But, all his waiting did not bear fruit as he did not turn up till mid-night. We were the last people to reach the temple that night and there was no possibility of the Trustee to come after this and the priest was also supposed to close the temple doors and go home to return next day early in the morning. We were indeed surprised at the turn of events. On our emerging from the temple, hot *'prasad'* was waiting for us outside, where the *sadhus* stayed. They insisted that we should take *'prasad'* there. It was excellent preparation and we were hungry. We had the food, thanked them profusely and left for Bhanjanagar.

Throughout our journey back that night and later till date I am intrigued as how this happened? I was directed to turn left, made to offer flowers and *pooja* besides partaking hot *'yagna prasad'* with my family without any effort on my part to do so. This sounds like a miracle, but it is true.

———— ·••♦♦•· ————

263

46

ORDERED TO STOP

When I was going to the Banadurga Complex in a thick patch of natural forest at the eastern end of small town of Kabisurya Nagar in drizzling rain and having *darshan* of the deity, the horn of my jeep, parked about 100 meters away on the highway blared. Sanyasi our old driver called aloud "Sir, the jeep is ready to move. Please come back".

It was Vana Mahotsava in July first week, 1980, when we were celebrating ceremonial tree planting all over the country. The Rambha Railway Station was celebrating the function as an enthusiastic Public Works Inspector had forested the railway land through planting of saplings around the station through his own effort. I went to attend the same with Sri N.C. Bal, Working Plan Officer and my son Pinu (Sumit) also accompanied us as his school was closed on that day. Usually when I pass through Kabisurya Nagar, I stop at the entrance to the Banadurga Shrine and walk about one hundred meters for a *darshan* (paying obeisance to the deity). But, as we were getting late for the function, I decided to skip visit to the shrine and planned to go to the deity on our return in the evening. It was a nice function at the railway station and I was very pleased to see the work of a railway officer and decided to write to his superiors to recognize his work and to suitably reward him.

After the function I did some other official work in Kodala range and returned in the evening through the same route. It started drizzling as we approached Kabisurya Nagar. We knew that we shall get drenched if we stop and walk to the shrine and return. Hence we paid our obeisance to the deity from the vehicle and wanted to proceed. The jeep stopped automatically at the entrance of the shrine with the engine refusing to start, Sanyasi our old driver said, "Sir, I cannot say why the vehicle has stopped. Let me see". He got down and opened the bonnet. I got down from the jeep and asked others also to get down and walked to Banadurga as Sanyasi tried to revive the engine. We ran to avoid getting drenched. Had a good *darshan* and a round (*parikrama*) of the deities, surrounded by a well preserved tree and vine grove. As soon we completed the *Parikrama* (perambulation), Sanyasi pressed the horn and called us to return as the vehicle had zoomed to life. We rushed back to find the vehicle in perfect shape, without any malfunctioning. We again did *pranam* to the deity and sat on the jeep on our return journey.

The event cannot be logically explained. But it was true. I felt that some unseen hand stopped our jeep so that our promised visit to the shrine must take place. I shall ever remember the incident as long as I am alive.

———————— ·◆◆◆◆· ————————

47

INTELIGENT PACHYDERMS

I had retired more than two years back as Chief Wildlife Warden and was visiting Jharkhand State as a Member of the Steering Committee of Project Elephant. I was camping at Jamshedpur, the famous Steel City of South Jharkhand and was looking for solutions to the severe human-elephant conflict in the region. While the problems were known, I wanted to have a first hand knowledge about a village where elephant depredation had recently taken place and wanted to talk to the people there. All senior officers both of territorial and wildlife wings of the department located there and few senior officers from state capital were there with me along with field staff.

We got information that a herd of elephants had raided a village not very far from Jamshedpur. The local range officer led the entire team to that village. I do not remember the name of this village, which was located on the eastern side of road leading to Ranchi. It was a fairly large village which looked quite prosperous considering the status of other nearby villages. There were hills on the south and west of the village, which were part of northern Easten Ghat hill range.

On our reaching the place, as usual, the village children led us to a *pucca* farm house flanking the farm with a live hedge as fence. Some vegetables were also raised there. It was house of a professor named Prof. Soren, teaching in a college perhaps in Jamshedpur or nearby.

He was a perfect gentleman and when we were introduced to him, despite losses he had sustained due to the raid by elephants, he led us to the place where elephants came the previous night.

It was a big hall used as granary, where number of sacks of harvested paddy was stored. A big hole was opened from the outside and bags of paddy were dragged out and eaten by the herd. Some paddy was lying scattered all around. If their version was to be believed, I was told that after making this opening with the tusks of the tusker, a young elephant of about five years of age was pushed inside by the herd. He pushed the bags of paddy one by one for ease of removing from the granary. Then the herd had a good feast for over two hours before departing to nearby degraded Sal forest patch as people started shouting at the day break.

It must have hurt Prof. Soren and his family. But they were quiet and were showing the damages as they knew that this is a high level team and shall be able to find some solution to the frequent problem of depredation by the elephants in the area.

As I was asking the details to the eye witnesses and other villagers, suddenly a burly bare bodied man in khaki shorts appeared from nowhere. He shouted at the top of his voice in Hindi, *"Yeh Bharat Sarkar Hai. Hum Bharat Sarkarko Nahin Chhodenge"*, meaning "He is Government of India and we shall not leave the Government of India".

He was pointing out to me as I was from the Project Elephant of the Ministry of Environment and Forests of Government of India. Everyone present was embarrassed and did not know what to do. Almost entire village had gathered around us and no one dared to confront that heavily built man with big mustches. It was only eight in the morning, but he was fully drunk and was not in his senses. He was incoherent while shouting and there was strong smell of country brewed alcohol emanating from his mouth. We were virtual captives as no one from the village interfered.

In the pretext of examining the foot prints of the elephant herd, I quietly walked into the farm, away from the crowd, with the local Range Officer following me, while the senior officers, who were standing there along with all subordinates in uniforms, were patiently listening to his abuses and were trying in vain to pacify him. Our vehicles were parked about 300 meters away on the main village road.

As I was pretending to measure the foot prints, I quietly asked the R.O. if he knows the contact details of the Officer-in-charge of the local Police Station. He replied in the affirmative. I asked him to tell our position and request the officer-in-charge to come with force. He did that. No one in the village could hear about their conservation.

I returned back to the scene of occurrence and talked to Prof. Soren, other villagers and senior officers without showing any sign of worry while the intoxicated man continued to hurl abuses at us and told us to capture the elephants or else they will capture us.

This went on for good two hours, when the O-in-C reached with his full armed force in two vehicles and rushed to the site and took the drunken man to custody, as he was still shouting. He saluted me and requested me to leave the place as he assured to handle this man appropriately.

After this we visited almost the entire district, including the Dalma Sanctuary and talked to the people and decided on location specific steps to protect elephant population there, while preventing human-elephant conflict to the extent possible, with the full participation of local people.

Most steps suggested were implemented fast as people were suffering from loss of life and property and elephants were either injured or killed. Even an elephant had killed a morning walker inside Tata Steel City.

The Jharkhand Government organized a seminar at Ranchi about a year after this incident where I was also invited. The affected people were also called. They informed us that most recommendations like photo-voltaic fencing, in charge of village community, raising alternate non-edible crops, well trained and equipped anti-depredation squads had yielded good results and the depredation has come down drastically in these affected areas.

I am sure with awareness of people, improvement of elephant habitats and linking of elephant habitats with proper corridors; men and these beautiful animals can live in harmony. These steps and many more innovative ones can save the Central Indian Elephant population. Of course, any anti-depredation measure without improving the natural habitat shall be futile as we cannot keep these massive pachyderms starved all the time without retaliation from them.

———————— ·•••••· ————————

48

TIGER IN THE CAMP

It was a moonlit night in the forests on the foothills of Gandhamardan hill range in Balangir district when I was awaken by a feral dog pushing its way into the leaf hut with a low whine.

It was last week of March, 1966. I was a young forest probationer who had passed out from the prestigious Indian Forest College, Dehradun less than a year before. As in charge of Khaprakhol range, I was required to align a forest road along the lower slopes of Gandhamardan. Forest roads were means of transporting forest material including timber and facilitate visit of the forest officers in petrol driven left hand drive Willys jeeps. Since forest roads often pass through difficult hill terrine lot of skill was involved to align a proper road with easier gradients for smoother movement of vehicles.

I had selected a perennial hill stream bank to set up my camp for the road alignment. Those days the road alignment equipments used to be very simple; consisting of prismatic compass, ghat tracer, Abney's level, Guntur's chain and

271

measuring tape besides Survey of India topographical map sheets prepared decades back after painstaking detailed survey. It took several days to align a 5 Kms road on hilly terrain. It used to be strenuous work to find a path with reasonable gradient (slope) for ease of movement of jeeps and trucks, on rocky hill slopes, passing through thick vegetation, precipices and big boulders. The alignments done by old time foresters, which used to be so good that many of them are even now being used as highways in many forested states of India, particularly in the Himalayas.

The camp consisted of two leaf huts one for myself, made of freshly cut brush wood. Furniture in my hut consisted of a foldable camp cot of canvass, a makeshift table made of freshly cut poles, which served all purposes like reading, writing, shaving and dinning. The next leaf hut was slightly bigger, placed about 5 meters away from mine and served as kitchen and accommodation for other staff and few labourers. The only contact with outside was a transistor radio (*sharp jhankar* make), I had bought to hear news broadcasts by the All India Radio or radio Ceylone broadcasting popular Hindi songs. As we had to stay for few days the fresh green leaves which formed the walls started wilting and drying up and through the openings then created the surrounding landscape and the pool in the stream flowing in front of my hut was clearly visible in the bright moon light. It was a very pleasing scene.

Suddenly almost at mid night, a stray dog started making a low sound 'kuun.......kuun.........kuun.........' and pushed its way into my hut. I got up and wondered why this dog which normally slept outside and ate food provided by the cook pushed its way in. Is it too cold outside? I did not feel so. In that case he could have chosen to enter the other hut which was warmer as there was fire lit there for cooking. After entering, instead of lying down, he was standing and looking outside through the openings in the wall, with his tail tucked between his hind legs.

I also peeped through the openings in anticipation of seeing some wild animals, which might have come to drink water from the stream.

A few minutes passed and suddenly a huge tiger, with its dark stripes on its tawny coat appeared on the bouldery bank of a pool in the stream. It quietly drank as much water it needed to drink and walked back to the nearby forest through the opening between the two huts. It was a majestic animal with a large head and wide stripes. Perhaps it was a male tiger. Of course, till then I had not seen a tiger in the wild.

I waited for about 15 minutes before opening my door and calling others in the next hut. I told them what I saw. They did not believe at first. But when they saw water that fell on the boulders from the body of the tiger and the terrified canine, they were themselves very scared and few offered to come to my hut for giving company. I did not need, as I knew that, he was not interested in humans. Otherwise he would have stayed there as he would have got our smell as a tiger's olfactory senses are very strong. Tiger does not go after humans and other slow moving animals like cattle unless it is old or injured or had acquired habit of man eating. Those days wild herbivores were plentiful, in tropical forests for tigers and leopards to prey upon. But man eating tigers were common in many parts of the country, where prey base used to be low. Even some of our seniors told that in earlier days promoting an officer to the rank of Divisional Forest Officer was based on his skill of shooting down a man eater.

We got up next morning and explored the nearby forest road and trail and found the pug marks of a huge tiger.

We camped there for few more days and were more cautious and got our hut walls repaired with freshly cut branches to prevent entry of dogs etc. Of course the large cat did not come again though we continued to camp there for few more days.

LEGENDARY SRI CHOUDHURY

Gudgudia, a valley in Similipal Tiger Reserve; is a very favorite camp site of the forest trainees of all the institutions of the state and neighboring states. The Forest Rest House there is also frequently used by foresters and other state officials while on tour to Similipal, the first Tiger Reserve of the state. Its proximity to West Bengal and Bihar (now Jharkhand) made it quite popular among the tourists too.

I was posted as Assistant Conservator of Forests at Rairangpur in Mayurbhanj district in 1966. It was in January, 1968 when Sri H.N. Sahu was the Chief Instructor of Mooney Forest School at Angul came on a tour to this Tiger Reserve with his trainees. It was severe winter in Mayurbhanj district and it was more severe in Similipal.

Sri Sahu and other instructors had reached Similipal for the field tour and practical exercise of the trainees of the school. I also accompanied the team to see that the field trip goes on without any hitch.

We had a long day showing the trainees different activities, acquainting them with different plants, structures and discussing different forestry techniques. Though the sylvan surroundings were very inviting and the cascading waters of hill streams full of *Mahasheer* fishes was rejuvenating, the day long activity was rather tiring.

On return to Gudgudia Forest Rest House, we had cups of hot tea and spent some time near the British type fire place located in the dining room of the 2-suit F.R.H. We fell asleep after a good dinner, tucked under our blankets. It was deep sleep due to preceding days tiring schedule.

I got up around 6.00 am and tried to tip toe out of my bed in order not to disturb Sri Sahu as he was deep asleep. The other suit was also occupied by other instructors.

I very cautiously opened the door in order not to make any noise to go out for a stroll around the rest house in the ozone rich morning air.

But as I opened the door and was about to step out, I saw someone draped in a blanket lying next to the door. Had I been slightly careless, I would have stepped on him. I stepped back. But that disturbance was perhaps enough to wake him up. A person in jungle green came out of the blanket. It was Sri Saroj Raj Choudhury, the first future Field Director of Similipal Tiger Reserve and a legendary forester.

I wished him and before I asked him anything, he told me that he reached from the field at around 2.00 am and learnt that we were sleeping. He did not like to disturb us and slept on the floor of the verandah with his field dress on with just a blanket to protect him from the severe cold. We were astonished to learn that he was touring in that cold night up to 2.00 AM, in his canvas topped Willy's jeep.

We were all surprised with the simplicity of this legendary forester who was responsible for starting scientific wildlife management training in India. A crack marks-man in his younger days, he was a very practical wildlife manager and forester. He was extremely daring and the father of pug mark method of tiger census. His research on Khairi, the tigress and many other wild animals he kept together in his rest house-cum-residence at Jashipur unraveled many facets of wild animal behaviour, hitherto unknown to zoologists. Among many other daring acts, he was responsible for capture of a wild tusker 'Agasthi' through chemical immobilization, the first in the world, only a year before his scheduled date of superannuation. He had caught a King Cobra, the most venomous snake with his bare hands. He was so caring for the wild animals that he even made a shoe for a wild elephant that had badly injured his fore leg. Though a very hard task master, he was a very affectionate person in heart. If any of his lower subordinates suffered from any ailment, which were quite common, he would personally look after them. All senior officers who were trained by him or who worked with him admit that they have not seen any forester of the country who can equal him in knowledge, guts, dedication or affection towards his subordinates while unsparing when it came to doing a job. For the first time ever, he established that no pug mark of

277

any two tigers or leopards are identical and based on that, he was the first to develop the pug mark method of census for tigers and leopards. His command over the English language despite being a student of science and afield forester was unparallel. His daily tour diaries were a treat to read. His book 'Khairi The Beloved Tigress', published 18 years after his premature death in 1982 is a master piece. All those who were trained by him, whether retired or very few who are still serving, treasure very fond memories of him as a very simple, unassuming, loving and practical teacher. Any superlative to describe him will definitely be an understatement. He was posthumously awarded *Padmashri*, a national honour, in recognition of his work on wildlife conservation. Unfortunately he died of heart attack while still in service.

50

THE COUNTRY THAT IS NO MORE

The impregnable wall separating East Germany (German Democratic Republic) from the West Germany (Federal Republic of Germany), 'The Berlin Wall' was still standing tall; artificially separating the people of the same country. While the western part was prospering, the eastern part, which was part of the communist block was impoverished and was mainly dependant on its agriculture or coal mining. All its contacts with the outside world other than East European Countries were through Moscow or other cities of Russia.

Dr. Biswanath Gupta who was the Director of M.C. Zoological Park (Chhatbir Zoo), Punjab and I, then heading the Nandankanan Biological Park, Odisha were nominated to visit the zoos of GDR for a month on a cultural exchange programme. Few incidents of that memorable visit have made our visit still more unforgettable.

We took an afternoon Air India flight to Moscow to take a connecting Aeroflot flight to East Berlin from there as there was no other convenient flight from other European metros. Though our flight landed on time in the evening, we could not take the connecting flight and had to stay in Moscow airport for the entire night.

As we waited for our flight and were quite hungry, we were happy to see a large group of young men looking like Indians sitting together. I heard then speaking in Bengali. I could understand and communicate in Bengali, though not so fluently. When I asked them where they were coming from, they were jubilant to find someone speaking their language and replied that they were laborers from Bangladesh and are on their way to Tripoli, Libya. Though they had arrived there about 8 hours back, they neither knew when shall be their next flight, nor did they have any food. No one understood their language. They did not have Roubles or sufficient Dollars to buy some food.

We saw their plight and took them in to the Station Manager's room of Aeroflot and requested to inform us when their and our flights are scheduled to depart, give us accommodation, food and inform about our baggage. Understanding their problem they issued 18 food coupons for dinner in the airport restaurant and showed us our baggage and returned our tickets with endorsements for issue of boarding passes.

But there was no luck with accommodation as they told that all hotel accommodations near the airport were fully occupied. They told that we were to spend the night in the airport. He asked us to listen to the airport announcements for the next flight check in.

We had no way other than to pull chairs to lie down, of course after some food. The Bangladeshis profusely thanked us for providing food and helping them. There were several hundred people from different nationalities who spent the night there. Some Japanese young men found it funny and were clicking their cameras around, perhaps to show, how bad the situation there was. However, at around 4.00 am we were called to report for the flight to Berlin. Fortunately there was English announcement. The Tripoli flight was also to depart little ahead of ours. We advised the young men to proceed to their assigned gate. It was not so very eventful other than that there was no water available for drinking, though Russian liquor was flowing in the Aeroflot flight.

Fortunately our hosts, Berlin Zoo, sent their Curator, Mammals to receive us and take us to the largest hotel of the city, Hotel Stad Berlin and we were accommodated in the 21st floor. We were given a very Senior Interpreter Ms Iva Iceman, who was very experienced and knew some previous Indian visitors to that country. It was impossible to communicate with anyone without an interpreter outside Berlin, though some Berliners understood English. We were to visit 9 zoos during our 1 month program. Besides, we decided to visit West Berlin Zoo on our own as it was out of bounds for GDR citizens.

Rostock was a nice little port city on the Baltic Sea. The Director wanted to entertain us in a famous restaurant of the city. All the tables were usually booked much in advance, otherwise it was impossible to get a seat. We reached on time. But to the dismay of Dr. Gupta, it was a fish restaurant and most dishes were of sea fish. But Dr. Gupta was averse to fish and had never taken fish due to fear of its bones. He said, "I shall not take anything." I told him that this would offend the host as he had made considerable effort to arrange a dinner there. As our host went out for a while, I told him in Hindi that nothing will happen to him as there is only one bone in the fish served, which can be easily removed. Still he was very reluctant. Finally he relented. He told me with all seriousness, "Partner, I shall take this as you say that nothing will happen. But, if at all I die here, due to the bones, you don't leave my body here, and take it back to India." We had a hearty laughter. Very cautiously he started eating the fish dishes and relished it very much.

For visit another small zoo we had to travel by train with our interpreter. It was cloudy and pretty cold though it was month of April. The coaches were heated with steam passing through metal tubes. The Director was quite hospitable and invited us for tea. Along with other dishes he served a few bananas. As it was cold we took some dishes and coffee but did not touch bananas. Someone had come to meet the Director, and he went out of the room for few minutes. Iva told us to take the bananas. We said to her that we won't as it was quite cold. She explained that the Director must have put in a lot of effort to get bananas here as they are imported from tropical countries and is served only in the 5-star hotels. Hence, he may feel offended. When we didn't show much interest, she took all of them and put them in her hand bag for consuming during the return journey, before our host came back into the room.

Dr. Gupta was very good at field botany. As we were going round the campus of Berlin Zoo with the Curator of Plants, he kept on asking her about different species. I was walking few steps behind and was enjoying the sylvan surroundings. Inadvertently, I made some bird calls, which I did practice from my early service career in Similipal forests of Odisha, a Tiger Reserve, where I used to attract wild birds while taking my packed lunch near a stream and rested a while.

Suddenly, their serious discussions stopped and they looked all around to the tree branches. She was an avid bird watcher. I asked her as to what happened? She said, "I heard a bird call. But this bird has never been reported from this area." I turned myself back and again made the sound. She had a hearty laughter and asked me to demonstrate that to her other colleagues, when we return back to the zoo office.

———— ✦✦✦✦✦ ————

To avoid pork, horse meat or beef, I decided to go vegetation during the entire trip, except in the fish restaurant. I learnt how to order for vegetarian dishes. In German, it was called *'gemuse platte'*. I used to tell them that while ordering food. Hence they used to give me lots of boiled cabbages, carrots, potatoes with salt, paper and some sauce to eat, of course with some bread and milk. The Director, Leipzig Zoo saw this. He was an old man of nearly 70 years and took us for a site seeing of the city and to the coal mining area. When we went to a plateau, we saw rows and rows of poly houses covering entire landscape of mined out area on the lower slopes with no sign of coal dust unlike our coal mining areas. I asked him what these small huts were. He told me jokingly that those were green houses where all their vegetables are grown and by the time I leave the country, I would have robbed all of them of the vegetables as I am constantly ordering for them. Of course, I was pleased to see these reclamation efforts, though it was economically a poor country. This zoo incidentally was a very old iconic zoo and the international stud book keeper for Bengal tigers.

As our hotel was located in a central place in Berlin we decided to go out for dinner in a restaurant. As usual, we left hotel at around 9.00 pm. When there was still sunlight and some boys and girls were in the parks. Some kept on photographing. We thought that it was early for dinner, as sun was yet to set. But, we found that all the restaurants were closed. We were surprised and were worried about our food. An African gentleman was observing us and came to us and asked if we were looking for dinner. We replied in the affirmative. Then he asked if we were new there and from India. We nodded. He told us that there people finish their dinner by 7.00 pm in summer months and shut their doors and windows, draw the curtains to prevent entry of sunlight and go to bed very early. He was kind to us and led to the only restaurant in the vicinity that was still open and advised us to finish dinner before 7.00 pm during our stay in that country, if we wanted dinner outside the hotel.

The Director of East Berlin Zoo was well past his 80 years and had been the Director of the zoo for almost half a decade. His son who was already quite old was one of the curators. He told me that, one who can prove himself in a technical position retires only when he becomes physically or mentally incapable of working. He was very popular in the zoo and was held in very high esteem by the local administration, to the extent that he can park his car at places only meant for high dignitaries of the city.

————————— ••••••• —————————

Dresden was a lovely little city with its forestry university at Tharand on the nearby hills. These hills are nick named as 'Switzerland of Germany'. The Director of the zoo was a nice person who had visited India and our zoo earlier. As we were sitting and discussing in his office, a very old lady walking with support of walking stick came in and handed over a cheque of 80,000 GDR marks and told the Director to use the money for the improvement of the zoo with a request to inform her if he needs any more money. They had a chat in German. After she left the office, the Director told us that she was a KGB (Russian spy agency) Agent and had retired long back. She has surplus money to spare out of pension she receives. As she loved animals, she chose to donate whatever possible to the zoo. People in other countries should emulate such examples and help in conservation efforts of different governments in order to ensure that with their survival our world becomes a better place to live in.

During our stay in GDR we had visited a village, where concrete models of prehistoric animals, birds, reptiles and some insects were constructed. A person had started this work almost 30 years back and has constructed large number of such statues of their original size. His exhibits were spread over a very large tract of land of more than hundred hectors and he had handed it over to his village community. It was a big draw for the tourists. As we visited it on a Sunday, the parking lot was packed to its capacity and for about 1 km the vehicles were lined on one side of the approach road. Such private enterprises are rare in our subcontinent except in few religious institutions.

We were fortunate to cross over to West Berlin being non Germans (GDR). Of course train operated between the 2 parts with very tight security. We had our passport and VISA valid for West Germany too. They were official passports. We saw the striking contrast between two halves of the same city with the west being so vibrant, bustling with economic activities. As we did not have much time there, the first destination was the zoo. We did inform its Director unofficially about our program. He, who married a Vietnamese lady was very hospitable and showed us his small but beautiful and well kept zoo, which was devastated during the 2nd World War. He was fluent in English. In one of its enclosures, I found some little Indian cows. I was surprised and asked him why they kept cows? He told that even in your country you are fast loosing these pure bred cows to hybrids and one day you will find none. This is an insurance against that. He hosted an Indian lunch for us with his senior zoo personnel. We made a few purchases of West German goods paying in US dollars as the products of GDR were of very poor quality. Return was also through very tight security screening. As we came out of the railway station, several people followed us and asked us if we had Deutsche Marks. They were willing to pay any amount in their currency, as that currency had hardly any value in any other western country. Only one little car, 'Trabants' was visible there against host of cars like Mercedes, Volkswagen, Fiat, Ford etc in West Berlin roads. They had their own airline operating flights to East European Countries and planes were all Russian made, guzzling fuel.

———————— · ♦ ♦ ♦ ♦ · ————————

Educating the school students on different conservation issues of wildlife was given a thrust in all GDR zoos. For this purpose they had set up 'zoo schools' in zoos with a Zoo Educator in charge. All schools around the city where members of this school and students of one class visited the zoo for half a day with their biology teacher and went round the zoo and asked her all questions they had about different aspects of ecology etc and all questions she could not satisfactorily reply, they would get the answers from the Zoo Educator who was equipped with films, charts, posters, animal parts and other equipments to remove their doubts. There were also guided zoo visits for different groups taken by the Director, Curators or Zoo Keepers on different days at different times for which the group paid an additional charge. Thus the zoo played a very important role in educating all sections of society on different conservation issues. The trained and licensed guide system in Nandankanan Zoological Park started in eighties, as the first such Indian zoo, has served similar purpose for large number of visitors, besides helping in reducing teasing and vandalism in the zoo. Few other institutions in India are trying this differently.

———————— · ♦ ♦ ♦ ♦ · ————————

Few species of animals have been brought back from the brink of their extinction like Prezwalski horse, Arabian Oryx, Pare Davis deer and European bison. Though European bison was extinct from most European countries, very few animals had survived in the wild in Poland. A bold decision was taken by the conservationists and they captured the entire lot for conservation breeding there and the number grew. Some of them were brought to GDR, a former range country, for such purpose. We had opportunity to see the ranch where all efforts were being made and care was provided for breeding them. From 3, their number had reached 14 when we saw them and they were planning to release them in the wild. As far as our country is concerned all the three Indian crocodilians owe their survival to the conservation breeding effort made for the 3 species. Efforts are on for Sangai, Red Panda and Snow Leopard too besides many other endangered species like hoolock gibbon, clouded leopard, vulture and Blythe's tragopan besides great Indian bustard to reestablish them in their own habitats.

———————— ◆◆◆◆◆ ————————

Despite difficult economic conditions, the people and government were keen to protect their monuments and heritage structures. Many of them which have been badly affected due to different factors including bombing in the Second World War, were being restored at considerable cost through Polish restorers who are supposed to be the best in East Europe in restoration work.

Another fascinating aspect was protecting the structures damaged by bombing in the 2nd World War. Few of them in cities have been retained in the same condition as ruins along side swanky modern structures, to remind their people of the horrors of war.

––––––––– ✦✦✦✦✦✦ –––––––––

All good things do come to an end. Our simple but interesting trip finally came to an end. Our hosts had paid us some money in their currency as *per diem*, which we did not need to spend except for some food items or few purchases of local stuff from their super markets. We were told that GDR currency has simply no value outside that country. Hence we asked our hosts for suggestion. They told perhaps only things which were worth taking from there were chocolates and coffee. We exactly did so except keeping few coins as mementos and bed very emotional farewell to our hosts and Eva, our interpreter to return again through Moscow and Delhi, flying over Hindukush Ranges and Afghanistan from where Akbar had once come to India to establish Moghul Empire in 1526.

––––––––– ✦✦✦✦✦✦ –––––––––

Now the wall *Berliner mauer* is no more. The infamous wall that was constructed in 1961 has been brought down in 1989. Both parts have merged into single Germany and the eastern part is making rapid strides to equal with its western part. It is heartening to note that the German Chancellor (equivalent to our Prime Minister) Angela Markel hails from the eastern part.

––––––––– ✦✦✦✦✦✦ –––––––––

51

INTOXICATING ORANGE SQUASH

Koira, tucked away in a remote corner of Sundargarh district of Western Odisha is now a bustling township full of hectic activities centered on its rich mineral resources of iron ore. It is still surrounded be fairly well clothed hills puck marked by pockets of dug out mines and dump yards. The trucks and other earth movers, the labour force and their hectic activities with red dust generated due to their movement makes life difficult for people to live there. But the affluence created due to these mining related activities is clearly visible through the shops, hotels, other buildings and expensive S.U.Vs. There is hectic activity round the clock.

But it was quite a different Koira decades back in early fifties with no place to stay even for a visiting government officers on duty and obviously hardly any official visited this remote corner. Malaria, which was quite common, deterred officials further. One had to pop very bitter Quinine pills every day to prevent malaria attack which used to be quite severe. The approach from the sub-divisional town of Bonai Garh was rather difficult though rugged terrain passing through thick forest teaming with wild animals including elephant herds.

Even a large river had to be crossed by boat. Canvas hooded, four-wheel drive petrol driven Willy's jeeps used to be the only means of transport for touring officers. Of course, the foresters ventured to come to this place occasionally as the area boasted of finest Sal forest of the region. Sal is a common timber species which enjoyed good market as a construction timber in the eastern, central and parts of northern India.

For any government officer visiting the area in late fifties of last century the usual camping option used to be tents or leaf huts. Quite often leaf huts used to be preferred as it did not involve carrying of tents over long distances in head loads. Brushwood required to make leaf huts was plentiful in the area and local labour used to be very cheap as people used to be quite poor. This area was earlier a part of Bonai State that merged with Odisha in 1948.

There was a forest officer named Sri N.R.Sanyal who was posted to this forest division (Bonai) as Divisional Forest Officer. He was quite a jovial gentleman, with lots of humorous true stories in store, who was earlier the State Botanist for Mayurbhanj State, the largest of princely states to merge with Odisha. He programmed to visit Koira and accordingly the local tribal labourers were engaged to build the camp of leaf huts in the valley. The camp was being given finishing touches by the tribals under guidance of field staff when the DFO reached after visiting some forest areas. As he sat down to wipe his sweat and remove his putties that guarded against leaches, ticks and reptiles and take out his shoes behind his folding camp table, placing his sola hat on it, the tribal labourers, six of them who sat in front of the hut kept looking at him and observing his activities as he was a dignitary for the area.

At this point of time his orderly brought some water and orange squash and placed on the table. He slowly started sipping the yellow sweet liquid. The curiosity of the tribal sitting in front of him was aroused as they kept on observing with fixed gaze. Sri Sanyal asked them in Odia "will you take this drink?" Pat came the reply from the eldest member," It is foreign liquor (alcohol) and we cannot take that as it is too strong." In this part of the country usually locally home-brewed *'handia'*, a rice beer or liquor distilled from *Mohwa* (a local forest tree) flower is consumed as intoxicant. Its colour was different from the orange squash.

Sri Sanyal assured them that it is tasty and shall do them no harm and asked the Orderly to give each of them some squash. As there were not enough glasses to give to so many people, cups were stitched out of Sal leaves using twigs as sewing material. These cups and plates made of these leaves are often used as disposable plates in this part of the country. *Siali* leaf, leaf of a climber is also used for this purpose. In later years small industries have stated mass producing such plates and cups and are widely being used in pick nicks and other get together even by affluent people as they are biodegradable.

Each of them was given a leaf cup and orange squash was poured in to it. They sipped it slowly with caution like they would do for *handia*. Sri Sanyal asked them, 'How do you feel." One of them replied, "rim===rim---rim" perhaps meaning tingling sensation. Slowly one by one they dosed off and lied down to deep sleep without bothering about the dignitary in front of them. Obviously, they felt intoxicated though it was plain soft drink. They were perhaps psychologically conditioned to accept it as a strong alcoholic drink as they thought that nothing other than high quality imported liquor can be served to a *Saheb,* as a senior government functionary being addressed those days.

Mr Sanyal mentioned to me this incident as I worked with him later in Bolangir while sitting near a fire place.

———————◆◆◆◆◆◆———————

52

THROUGH THE SEA ROUTE

The relatively calm waters of Paradeep Port harbor slowly gave way to choppy waters of the Bay of Bengal as our ship INS Ramadevi of Indian Coast Guards was towed through the navigation channel. Capt. Satpathy in his immaculate white uniform showed us around this small ship, its different facilities, navigational aids and other details. Sri S.C. Padhi, the Chief Wild life Warden of Odisha state and I were on a visit to see the preparedness of different organizations including ours to prevent harm to the Olive Ridley turtles as they come to nest in Ekakula Nasi, north of Paradeep in very large numbers. Indian Navy, Coast Guards, State Police, Fishery Department of the state and the district administration, besides our Forest Department were working together for the protection of these reptiles as it was the largest of the nesting grounds of the species in the world. After going round the ship we settled down on its deck as that gave us an excellent view of the surrounding sea as it was a bright sunny winter day. Our destination was the nesting ground; from where we were to take a river and land route back. Besides, staying on the deck saved us from the giddiness we would have experienced in the confines of the cabin.

We maintained fairly good distance from the shore in order not to hit ground as the ship needed good depth of water to navigate smoothly. But we had to remain as close as possible to the shore to see the activity of the fishing trawlers. We could see some boats on the radar screen of the ship, but they were quite in deeper waters and were not to harm the mating turtle pairs who normally stay closer to the shore. During those days Gahirmatha had not been declared as a Marine Sanctuary. It is possible that the boats could know about the Coast Guard ship's movement and avoided the shallow waters. We saw many pairs of turtles and some single females too.

But to go to the shore from the ship we needed a much smaller boat, which could navigate through the coastal shallow waters. But the Forest department did not possess any sea going boat as most of its activities were confined to the rivers and creeks of Bhitar Kanika sanctuary. Hence a private trawler was hired for us. We were in radio contact with the staff in that boat. Finally, based on our direction the boat could reach us by around 3.30PM. But, as the water was so choppy that, while the ship appeared to be still, the trawler was very unstable and was going up by about 2meters and dropping that much. Capt. Satpathy, directed the trawler to come to deeper waters in order to reduce this as it was almost impossible to descend to the boat without getting hurt or being thrown in to the sea. We travelled almost two Km deeper in to the sea. Before we attempted the descent, Captain tried it and tripped. He was worried about us as we were not at all experienced with such situation. He also explored the option of sending us down to the trawler's deck with rope ladder. But the heaving of the small boat to a considerable height every few seconds made that option too risky, as one could get crushed between the two vessels. We had good number of our staff in the trawler. He directed the little boat to come to the sea ward side of the ship. This, somewhat calmed the trawler, and the drop and rise reduced considerably, though still not felt safe for us. He directed our staff to stand on the deck of the boat and form a circle. He advised us to jump in to center of the human circle one by one, when trawler rose with the wave. Once on the trawler, he directed our staff to grab us so that we don't get thrown in to the sea or get crushed between the ship and the small boat. Sri Padhi jumped first followed by me. This worked and we left the ship thanking the crew of the ship profusely on a very choppy sailing back to the land to see the preparedness of our field formation there for protection of turtle eggs when laid from predators and the human interference.

Our staff faced many such situations on regular basis both in the rivers, land and coastal waters facing turtle poachers, inclement weather and difficult working conditions. They need support in terms of adequate man power, proper modern equipments, good mobility and better living conditions to make them more effective.

++++++

53

Trough A Circuitous Route

It was a pleasant February morning in 1975 when I with my family consisting of my very old father, wife Manju, three small children were driving up the hills of Baliguda of Kandhmal district in a private Fiat car of a friend. I had burrowed the car to go to Berhampur in south-east Odisha from Bhawanipatna in western Odisha. As the sun was coming up from the sides of higher hills on the east, the shadows of trees, sal, asan, kurum, dhaura jamun, mango and Kusum etc, part of the tropical forest was getting shorter. I was under transfer to Berhampur to take up the responsibility of afforestation division there. Children were savoring the beauty of the sylvan surrounding they were passing through. Of course, my father, a former forester and my wife, daughter of a senior forester of the state had seen lots of forests, though they were enjoying it.

At this juncture, Manju asked me as to why I changed the route suddenly and took a longer route suddenly turning left at the intersection. We had left Bhawaniatna around 4.30 AM, when it was still dark, so that we could reach Berhampur before evening through the shortest route called KV line, a distance of around 350 KMs of hilly road, through which I had never travelled before. Of course all our neighbors were up and saw us off stuffing eatables in the car for the children. We were to take breakfast at a place called Lanjigarh Road invited by our staff and lunch somewhere on the way. It was a Monday and on this day my father only took raw rice and vegetarian dishes prepared with cow ghee. So we carried some rice, vegetable etc and ghee for him to cook lunch wherever possible en-route. Our divisional staff bed us good bye on our divisional border. When we reached the road inter section from where the shorter road bifurcate, impulsively told the driver to turn left, a much longer and hillier route.

I told Manu that, it was familiar route and perhaps it will be easier for us to get the food for father cooked at G.Udaygiri Forest Rest House, while we can get some food from a hotel in this small town.

We reached that place around noon time and left the main road a proceeded towards the rest house. As we entered the campus, to our surprise, we found a uniformed staff running to the front of the FRH. I knew him well as Sarangi worked with me earlier. After wishing us he straightway requested us to get freshened up for lunch. I was completely taken by surprise and asked him if he had got the lunch prepared for some others, as I had not intimated my program to anyone else. He requested me to take lunch, most reluctant to reply to my question. I told him that we could take our food even from the hotel, but please ask someone to cook food for father and we were carrying the ingredients for the same. To that he said even lunch for him has been cooked as specified. This was still intriguing. It was a wonderful lunch and even the bed was ready for those needed to have a siesta. Father lied down.

I took Sarangi aside and asked him, how he could know about our change of route without our informing him. It was almost two decades before the arrival of cell phones. Hence there was no way for him to know my changed program. To that he said a senior forest officer accompanied by a judicial officer were to come there on tour and were scheduled to take lunch there. The judicial officer's lunch had similar specification like my father's. We were pleasantly surprised at the turn of events and the astonishing coincidence. We profusely thanked Sarangi and his staff for the excellent lunch, paid for the same and departed for Berhampur down the hill road.

It is is popular saying in Indian culture that 'on every grain of food the name of it's would be consumer is pre- written'. This perhaps happened in this case, making us to make a detour of several kilometers of circuitous route to take the food we were destined to it. This memory lingers on in memory of my entire family for more than forty years now.

54

YOUNG TUSKER OF BARBIL

It was a very hot May forenoon in the richest iron ore belt of India in the far north corner of Odisha state bordering the state of Jharkhand, where we were scanning a small valley and it's surrounding for an old tusker. Though it was around 9.00AM in the morning it had already become too hot to bear as the open cast iron ore mines all around without much vegetative cover was radiating heat. Summer was in its peak in the tropical landscape. Our entire team consisting of foresters, veterinarians and local guides were perspiring heavily.

We were on look out for a very old emaciated tusker with long tusks. He was not eating much and was too weak to walk any distance. Our intelligence input suggested that professional poachers were stalking this old bull to take these tusks for ivory to be traded in international market, where it fetched lucrative price. It became still easier as this was very close to the state borders and was much easier to commit a crime and escape to the other state, making it difficult for the law enforcing agencies to apprehend them. Hence in order to save the tusker we had decided to sedate him and de-tusk him so that the lure of ivory shall no longer attract the poachers or ivory traders. The forest department also planned to provide food supplement in order to facilitate easier feeding without having to roam long distances in search of forage. But to everyone's surprise, he was not seen anywhere. Perhaps to escape from intense heat he had taken shelter inside a thick vegetation thicket, where we could not spot him. We, particularly the local field staff were surprised. After about couple of hours of intensive search, we left the site; instructing the staff to inform us through very high frequency radio (VHF) when the tusker is sighted.

Around 3.00 PM the hand set came to life and there was an urgent message from the local Forester that the pachyderm has been sighted near the peak of a small wooded hill clothed predominantly with Sal forest. He was standing under a spreading *Ficus* (Banyan) tree. We rushed there without wasting any time as he could disappear again. We rushed to the sight with all tranquilizing drugs, gun and accessories. Heat was still unbearable. We went to the base of the hillock where he was standing. The Forester who had spotted him accompanied our team of about ten persons. I focused my binoculars through the opening in the thick vegetation. His shape was quite clearly visible. From that I could easily guess that he was a young healthy animal. As I expressed that to the team, the Forester who had been keeping an eye over the movement of the old tusker for the last fortnight or so asserted that this was the only animal in the area and there was no other in the vicinity. He insisted that we go closer. We advanced about fifty meters up the hill and now I became very sure that it was not the animal we were looking for.

I warned the team members that this young tusker might charge us if we go any closer. I told the team to stand its ground and shout together to scare him away. From that point onwards we inched forward up the hillock, while shielding ourselves behind trees in order not to provoke him to make sure that this was not the old tusker we intended to immobilize.

At this point he perhaps got our smell as he raised his trunk, let out muffled trumpet, broke a few braches and pushed a young Sal sapling down and started charging with raised trunk. All of us stood still and shouted in unison. He stopped after coming down by about twenty meters. He did not turn back though. His gaze was fixed on our team. The waiting game on either side went on for good fifteen minutes with none moving. Finally he started shielding himself behind some thicker vegetative cover to his left and started retreating while still keeping us in his view. We slowly retreated down the hill while maintaining visual contact with him. We were lucky to have escaped his wrath.

Had we not stood our ground as a group and ran away he could have chased us for intruding in to his space. He would have felt that he was being attacked and retaliated. Any such retaliation could have been fatal for some as all of us were not in the best of shape to out run a charging young bull. One must allow the minimum required privacy to wild animals and do not degrade their natural habitat. Like we humans every wild animal loves his/her privacy and always tries to guard it. Besides, for a wildlife manager it is essential to know the animal behavior before taking up any activity concerning a particular species, particularly those who can harm you when provoked. Even docile animals need to be treated with dignity. Let us try to provide this to them in the form of proper undisturbed habitat without our interference.

————— ++++++ —————

www.ingramcontent.com/pod-product-compliance
Lightning Source LLC
Chambersburg PA
CBHW070629290526
45790CB00001B/45